PEACE BY PIECE

Peace by Piece
Victoria Villasenor, Ed.
Global Words Press
Copyright retained by individual authors
Cover Image by Daniel Donson
Cover Design by NVoke Designs
Internal Artwork by Buster Fisher
Collection copyright © 2015 Global Words Press
Imprint Digital, UK
Cataloging information
ISBN: 978-0-9929354-5-0

PEACE BY PIECE

2015
GLOBAL WORDS PRESS
NOTTINGHAM, UK

CONTENTS

Preface	5
Acknowledgments	7
The Words He Said by Spirit Roc	11
Leave Out All the Rest by Catherine Lewis	15
Lost and Found by Cherie Rosann	23
Awakening by Nadia Stephens	29
Moving On by Anonymous	37
The Daughter. The Death. The Danger.	43
Labelled by A. Woman	49
Josey by Alex Mawson-Harris	55
Differences by Aisha	59
A New Life by Anonymous	61
You'll Turn Into a Chip by Iona Tamburrino	67
Boobs, Bosom, Tits by Kathleen Pollitt	77
Don't Give Up by Anonymous	85
One Way Ticket by Mina Fatemi	89
The Girl in the Rose Garden by Clare Barton	95
Sunday Dinner by Rastarella	103
Silence is Loud by Sarah	111
Reflections by TJ	115
Turning Point by Maureen Jeffs	121
An Old Brown Settee by Andrea Agacinski	129

Preface

Every woman has a story to tell. That's how the idea for this project began. Early in 2014, Nottingham Women's Centre began a new chapter in its own story. The Centre, established in 1971, had once housed a women's library. Packed to the rafters with feminist texts and hard to find books by women authors.

Over time, the library fell into a state of disuse. The books remained, gathering dust, but the library itself ceased to exist. When I arrived at the Centre in 2011, I was struck by the potential of the space. There is so much knowledge and experience contained within the pages of the books, and the raw history of the women's movement is told through the magazines and journals we hold, such as Spare Rib. The library had it all; it just needed life to be breathed into it and thanks to generous grants from various funders, including Awards for All (a Big Lottery fund), we were able to do this.

Alongside the physical redevelopment of the library, we felt it was important to contribute our own book to its shelves. Many of the texts we hold are from the 1970s and 80s and reflect on life for women as it was then. We wanted to share something of the voices of women today. I'm often asked, 'Who uses the Women's Centre?' There is no simple answer to this, other than to say that we are a centre for all women. Some women come to us at a crisis point in their lives, other women come to us because of a connection with the feminist movement, and some for no other reason than to be in a welcoming space with other women. Above all, these are the stories of women, women like you and me. Women who have lived, loved, lost, and survived.

~Melanie Jeffs, Nottingham Women's Centre Manager

Acknowledgements:

Projects like this one are a dream come true for a writer and editor. Not only do I get to hear poignant, personal stories, but I'm able to publish them for others. For this, I am truly grateful. A book like this can not be made without a team of people behind it.

First and foremost, thank you to each and every writer who participated in this project. Thank you for your courage and bravery, and for your words--words I am so incredibly proud to be able to print.

Thank you to the Nottingham Women's Center, who facilitated the project, and to Melanie Jeffs, whose constant optimism and support were always appreciated. And to Awards for All, for funding this wonderful project.

Much thanks to Dan Donson for the wonderful cover art, Nick Voke at NVoke design for the cover design, and Buster Fisher, who created the amazing illustrations to complement each story. Special thanks to Nicci Robinson. Without her keen eye and patience, this would be a very different book. And to those others who jumped in and helped make this possible: thank you.

You are all my heroes.

~Victoria Villasenor
Director, Global Words CIC

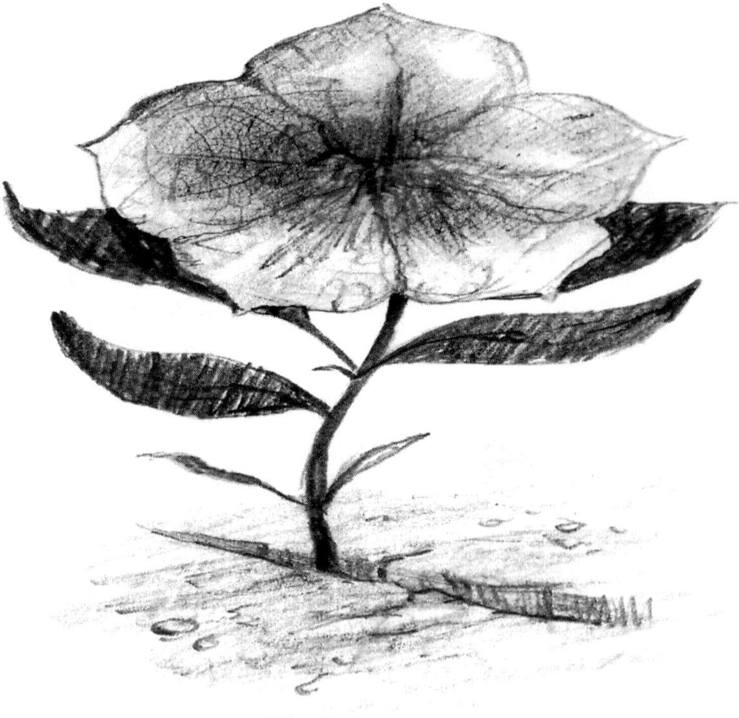

THE WORDS HE SAID
by Spirit Roc

If I would have listened to the words that my Pops once said, I would have never let him inside of my head, let alone inside my heart.

"Let no man so much as raise his hand in a reflection of his aggression in your direction, you're worth so much more. Let no man control you and what you want to do to get where you want to be; keep your eyes open and focused never walking blindly. If he loves you from the heart you'll never be apart, even if you're not together, but child I tell you this and my words you must hear, don't live with no man who brings nothing but fear. I swear it'll only destroy you!"

I'm sorry pops, I walked blindly eyes totally wide shut. I'm afraid to tell you I fear as I sit here nursing these cuts. You see, I thought he was my soulmate as it started out so right, I got lost in blinded love, blurring my vision and my sight. Now I'm crying into the night... will it happen again?

Convinced me it was my fault that caused his hand to raise and strike... "What are you like?" It happened again and again, became so hard for me to speak as his power and control had ground me down to weak.

You see, I was to blame for his many actions towards me, but how could it be when egg shells I walked on around him? I looked into his eyes prayed to the lord above, please make him stop this anger and be with us in love. In him I saw her, our little girl, and wanted him to be a part of our world as a strong family together. I held on for so long inside knowing it was wrong, in living hope his aggression would be gone, but in hope I would live forever. Then when I looked at her, our little girl, I knew he couldn't be a part of our world as I needed our daughter to grow strong and not accept his wrongs as right.

I can't have my daughters grow in a way that they think it's ok to be treated this way. I have to be their voice and have positive say in my actions. Plus and plus doesn't equal subtractions, meaning love plus love can't take away love and replace that love with negative actions. Destroying the mind and leaving hurt, pain and unhealthy implications for my children isn't love. I have to do what's right and follow my heart, and not the part that says "I love him" but the part that says "I love my children more, with unconditional love that's real and pure." A life we'll lead that's new, no hurt, pain or shame because it's not based around me and him or for the things I am to blame.

I chose to leave and walk out the door, I refused to let his pain affect us anymore. In his selfish mind he blamed me for his loss, not realising that it was at our cost. You see, life is something to be treasured, not measured by control and power. I should have never been his punch bag, but instead the seed to his flower. A flower he should have nurtured with love and allowed to grow from seed to bud, to blossom into that beautiful flower. With that, we would have held the power! He took that power and claimed it over me, blinding himself from being able to see that what he tried to mold me into, I already was.

You see he needed to let go of the fact we were no longer together and take heed of the life we'd created together in our little girl, who was no longer a part of our world, but a part of his and mine. He continued to abuse her with his criminal mind in continuing to abuse me through her. You see what he didn't realise is that our daughter offered comfort and love, a caring hug when my tears I could no longer hide. She looked in my eyes telling me, "Mummy it will be ok," even when those words I didn't have the strength to say to her. I thought I was protecting her by not allowing her to see, when in my eyes she had already saw. A confused mind, worried and scared, not understanding what it feared but knew it was fear and I wasn't there to take away the hurt and the pain because I allowed him to do it again and again. If I had kept her there in that same situation I was going to lose her, mind, body and soul, as I would have then become the abuser.

My love plus his love didn't equate to that of equal-ness, and my love plus his hate was not my fate either. In seeing the world through her innocent eyes a newness in life we had to seek to find, before my blindness was his very demise.

So Pops, I want to thank you for the words that you once said, that I held so strong and deep in my head. You inspired my flower to grow from seed to bud and blossom into that beautiful flower... Now I hold the very essence of my power!

'I have been through hell and back, have a heart that would give the devil heat rash. A warmth to make him forever regret his fall'

Sometimes true strength is not holding on to something, but the realisation that we should in fact be letting go.

REAL LOVE HOLDS NO PRISONERS!

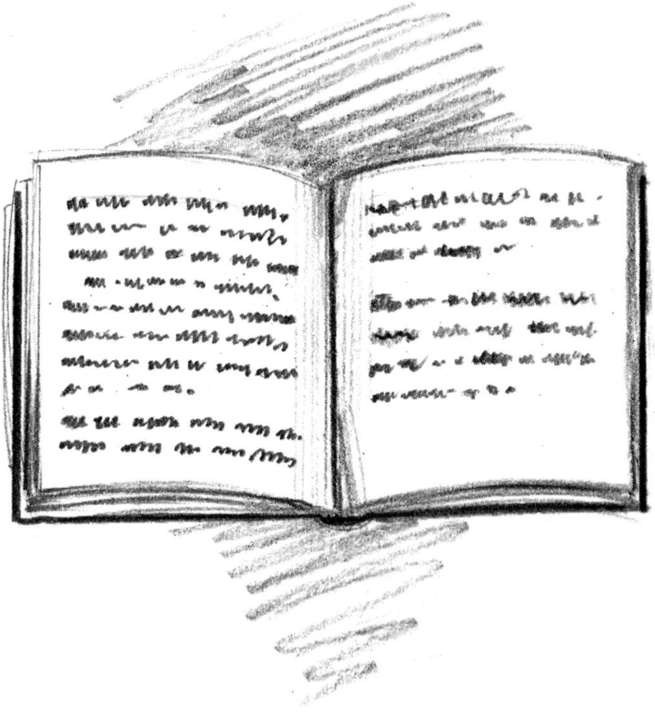

LEAVE OUT ALL THE REST
by Catherine Lewis

Miss Lewis?' A woman's voice penetrated the darkness, and I struggled to open my eyes. My eyelids burned and felt as if they were full of sand. A sliver of fluorescent light crept in, and they quickly closed again. I tried to speak, but my mouth was so dry all that escaped was a husky gagging noise. I felt my arm being raised, something squeezing it, and in alarm my eyes sprung open. Squinting against the light, I saw a blue uniform, and a small machine with numbers on it. A blood pressure monitor. That was the squeezing sensation. The nurse pulled the cuff from my arm, and wrote something down in her notepad.

I managed to croak, "What happened?"

She replaced the red folder at the foot of the bed, and paused for a moment. She stared at me, and then dropped her eyes. "Hm. Don't you remember?" she said, before striding away.

As I lay there, it came back to me. Part of it, anyway. I had no recollection of the ambulance, of arriving, or what had happened since, but what I did to bring myself there, I remembered that. As I pulled the sheet over my head and curled into a tight ball, I thought that my eyes still felt gritty, and could really use a tear or two. The problem was, I had none left. I stared into the darkness and prayed for sleep.

The following day was the ward round, which involved a hoard of medical students standing around me watching while a doctor bellowed, "Why are you here?" in full view of every other patient. They already knew why I was there, and I was good enough at humiliating myself, I didn't need any assistance. I refused to answer and was eventually discharged. I wandered out of the main doors and around the car park with bandages on my arms and a sore stomach. I had no idea where to go or what to do. I slumped down on a bench, next to a man with a broken leg.

    I hadn't washed for a few weeks. My arms were stinging from where I had pulled a Gillette blade over them. My stomach ached. My throat burned. The concoction of pills and vodka I had swallowed down hadn't done my insides much good. And the physical state I was in mirrored that of my mind.

    Sitting on the bench, huddled over, staring at the concrete, I considered my options. I had no job to return to. The week before the manager had called me in to tell me I had to resign or be sacked, because, "You need help, before you end up on the other side of the door." (Ironically enough I was working on a secure psychiatric ward at the time.) Although I knew she was right, it was devastating. My job was the thread of normality I had clung to. Look, I'm working, I'm ok!

    A few days after that, my relationship ended. Unable to take anymore of my erratic behaviour, my partner, sobbing and apologising, left me. I hold no grudges, I was difficult to live with. Nestled alongside my suicidal behaviour was extreme paranoia. I thought the government were watching the house, and I insisted on receiving an hourly phone call, 'So I know you're not dead'. Unfortunately the split meant I lost my home too, as we had shared a house. So, I was alone. Jobless. Homeless. And pretty mentally unstable. When things crash so spectacularly, the old saying, 'the only way is up', isn't just a cliché. I couldn't go any lower. Up really was the only way.

    The beginning turned out to be another trip to the psychiatrist. I shuffled into his room and sat down. The chairs in psych rooms are always those huge puffy ones. I think they're supposed to encourage relaxation in the hope that you'll talk instead of staring at the wall or at your shoes. In actual fact, the people who end up in that office are so uptight that they'll stiffen at any kind of attempted comfort. Hence, I resisted the chair's efforts to envelope me into its folds of pink fabric. I perched on the end, tucked my feet tightly underneath me, and clasped my clammy hands together.

"Hi, how are you?"

I broke eye contact with the swirly patterns on his carpet and stared at him.

He was a wiry man. Dark hair with flecks of grey, brown eyes, and a Southern accent. He always dressed well, and I could tell his suit was expensive. I bet he had a nice house. A driveway. Fresh tulips in a vase on the windowsill.

He smiled, and leant back easily, hands on his head.

"I'm fine."

This was my standard answer. It was easier to say. And I couldn't have explained even if I wanted to. I was tired. So tired. Not a sleepy kind of tired, but deep fatigue. It crawled into my bones and held me down, like a thick cloak of exhaustion.

I gazed at the carpet again, imagining myself shrinking, climbing down from the chair, and walking around the swirls. I zoned in now and again, caught him saying, "You can manage this..." and "...give you some structure." His words mingled together into one long hum.

Then suddenly I heard 'group,' and 'therapy.'

"What?"

"Yes. I recommend an intensive course. You'll be going 3 days a week, all day. It'll cover social therapy too."

I opened my mouth to protest, but fatigue answered for me.

I shrugged. "Fine."

I was on a waiting list for 8 months. The urge to give in to the constant suicidal thoughts was excruciating, but I am blessed to be quite a headstrong person, and when I say I'll do something, do it I will. It sounds so simple, writing that. It wasn't. Arguing with the instinct to swallow pills or step out in front of a bus is a war. An internal war. Even something as simple as using a knife to chop up an apple becomes an ordeal, because everywhere you see a way out. Just. One. Little. Cut. It'll all be over. But I held on. And eventually I got my letter with my start date. I walked up to the building, rang the bell, and walked inside.

Even today, almost two years later, I struggle to describe what it was like. We were like newborns in many ways. We all had serious issues, usually from childhood, and didn't really understand how to move through the world. In order to learn we had to go back. Remember. Feel. Live it all over again, minute by minute. Often it became too daunting, and one of us would disappear, retreat back to childhood coping mechanisms. One person used to grab a blanket and climb into the cupboard under the sink. Another would sit in the corner, thumb in mouth. Others sat in silence, blanking every effort to involve them. Many people left altogether, the strain simply too much.

I too, struggled with the process. I carried a dark secret. A self loathing that stuck to me like thick wet tar. My belief was that this world was better without me. That I offered nothing. I faced day after day after day of mundane worthlessness with no end to the gnawing emptiness. At first, I believed I was inherently evil. I believed there was something rotten inside me, and that feeling had started when I was around 5 years old. I suppressed it for years. I was careful never to let anyone near me, in case they found out. They had to be protected. As I slowly waded through my thoughts, repressed rage would hit me. Hatred on a whole new level. I walked around in constant burning pain. My head and jaw ached, my forearms would tingle, and I'd clench my fists continuously. In a desperate effort to release some of it I would go into the bathroom, lay on the floor, scream, and kick the door until I thought it would hang off its hinges. Then, totally spent, I would curl myself around the toilet, sobbing until I could no longer think or move.

The mind is an incredible thing, and will go to extraordinary lengths to protect us. But it can only take so much. Mine had been stretched as far as it could go, and now it had snapped. Things started to come back to me. Slowly at first...a flash here. A smell there. Not true, surely? This wasn't me, that didn't happen... except it did. It happened. To me. I began to realise what the evil inside really was. Guilt. I felt guilty. For something I had no control over. As a child I had no voice, I had no escape. All that pain, rage, disgust... turned inward. So when I began exploring the idea that it wasn't mine to have, it was a tricky process. I refused to accept it for a long time. I had a 'but' for every explanation. I had a subconscious need to self destruct. I would scream that I was leaving, that I wasn't crazy, I didn't belong there, my life had been fine, I wasn't a victim.

Then I'd go back, ready to reflect, and talk, and break through the next illusion.

Recovery from any trauma or mental illness is a long and difficult process. There aren't enough words here, or indeed that exist in the English language, to truly describe those times. Even now I have days where something unexpected will set me off. Something will send my mind rocketing backwards, and I'll suddenly be reliving a moment that has lain buried. I deal with it now. I can. Because I had a realisation. The realisation that changed my life. It was not my fault.

And that's what I want to say. That's why I'm here, in this book. If you read my story, and see yourself, I want to tell you, it wasn't your fault. Please, let that guilt go where it belongs. It is not yours to carry, and you deserve to be free. You are not tainted.

It isn't possible to change the past, nor what it leaves us with. There will be days when everything is grey, misty, and

Peace by Piece

just brushing your teeth is an effort. If you manage to climb out of bed at all, that is. Be assured, they will pass. Alongside the tough days, there will be days that remind you why it's worth sticking around. There are moments of liking what you see in the mirror. Moments of fizzy, pounding joy. Moments of "Wow, this life thing really is great!" Moments of anticipation for the future. If that all sounds too far fetched right now, that's ok. Just think of tomorrow. Or the next hour. Whatever it takes to keep moving forward. You will get there. There will be moments. Of you.

Peace by Piece

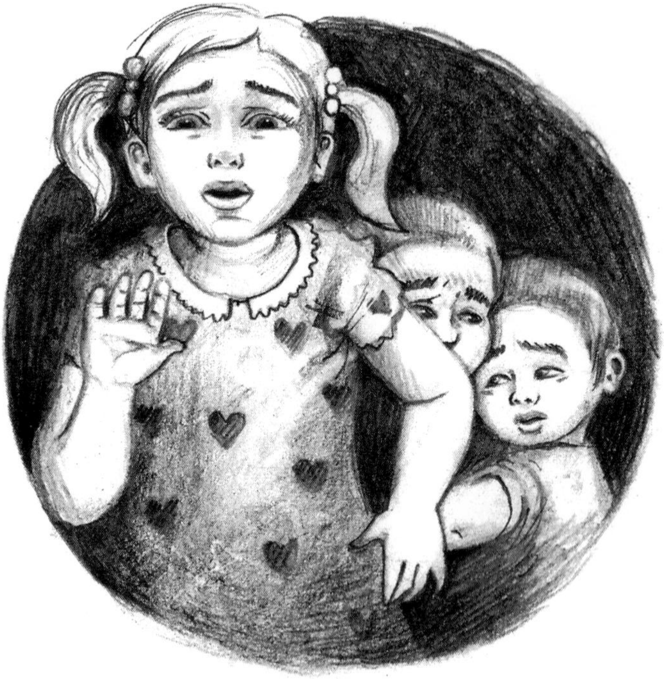

LOST AND FOUND
By Cherie Rosann

Who am I?
We see through the same eyes but she is not aware I'm here
I'm with her through all her joys, her sadness and tears
Once, long ago, she knew me and although she went away
I always stayed here to help her through each and every day
At times she caught a glimpse of me and came so very near
But then she would lose her way fighting anger, sadness and fear
I was there through all those times, a loyal and loving friend
Trying so hard to guide her, helping her to mend
I hope one day she'll find me, turning inwardly to see
Reflecting back out at her, Love, her eyes, her Self, me.
Who am I? I am her Self.

She is tired. She feels so old. Is she really only eight? She desperately wants to be loved, to feel safe and secure. To be a child for a while, embraced in the bosom of a happy family where her parents love and accept her for herself. She wants a peaceful, happy home where she can play with her dollies, sing, dance, and draw lovely pictures. She wants to express her feelings and she wants so much to enjoy going to school. But, it started as it always did.

She stared in horror, hearing the crash as her father threw her mother into one of the many kitchen cupboards. It was a tall cupboard with one door that was painted pale blue, like the sky on a crisp winter day where feathery clouds hang around waiting for the dark to descend upon the world. The floor was covered with pale blue linoleum, and a table and chairs stood in the centre of the big rectangular kitchen. Cupboards ran the length of one wall, topped by a bench that was decorated with dark blue tiles. The bench continued along under the windows, leading to the kitchen sink where louvers allowed a view out over the huge back yard. There was a stove situated between the sink and the back door, with a floral tea-towel over the handle of the grill. Next to the stove was the back door, and adjacent to this there were low benched cupboards along the wall that ended at the lounge room door. A refrigerator, redolent of the sixties, stood next to the hallway door. The kitchen windows, complete with screens to keep the mosquitoes and cockroaches out, were next to the tall cupboard and high off the ground on that side of the house. On that particular evening, they were thrown wide open, allowing the jewel coloured café curtains to flutter delicately in the evening breeze, a blessing after a hot, humid, summery day in that subtropical climate.

The generous yards were broken up by chain link fences. The families who lived in that vast housing estate were mostly middle class where the children attended the same school, played together at each others' houses and generally enjoyed their childhood.

This wasn't the case in that particular house. It witnessed a cruel, raging alcoholic yelling at her mother and inflicting his vicious nature upon she and her children, his own flesh and blood. Three little kids tried desperately to cope with a tyrannical man who bullied and oppressed them all. She heard the slap of his hand as it connected with her mother's arm.

She tried to appeal to her raging father. "Dad," she screamed, "leave her alone!" She's crying. She sees her mother sobbing after bouncing off the kitchen cupboard. He's looking at her, his beautiful little daughter, with hate filled eyes, his rage fuelled by alcohol and something else buried deep inside him. He advances with his hand ready to strike and snarls at her, "what are you crying about? I'll give you something to cry about!"

Peace by Piece

Her little brother and sister are standing near the doorway that leads from the kitchen into the short hallway, off which the three bedrooms and the bathroom are located. They're crying, her little sister is almost screaming. She must protect them. What else can she do? She hates him. She wants to hurt him, maybe even to kill him. She stands her ground, stepping in front of her little brother and sister to shield them from her violent father. She must protect them. She cannot protect her mother. Her mother, weeping as she leans against the tall, light blue kitchen cupboard, cannot even protect herself. Her father looks like he wants to kill them all. She cannot trust him and there is no one to help her. There is no Child Line, it's the sixties. There are no neighbours to come to her aid although they must surely hear the commotion coming from that house. There is no one to tell, not even the police. No safe haven. The terrible secret must stay within the walls of the prison that had become her home. She must be the protector, the little warrior. Stand your ground little warrior! For your survival and theirs, push your feelings down. Don't let him see you. He must not see you. Hide your fear. Hide your Self.

It was then that she lost her Self. Hidden away safely, to be protected for all time. She became a pleaser. It was the only way to survive. She tried to keep the peace as much as she could. She tried so hard to be a good little girl, to be her wretched father's confidante, to parent him during his intoxicated episodes where she endlessly endured his cruel jokes about her mother and her mother's family. She would keep her mood light, pacifying him, all the while wanting to run away, to escape. She packed her tiny case once, but only got as far as the front gate. Where would she go, what would she do? How would they survive without her? She listened to her mother's dislike of her father's family. She would hear her mother banging pots and pans, the car pulling into the driveway, the key turning in the front door and she knew

what the evening ahead was going to hold.
    Sunday would dawn and everything would be quiet. Normality descended upon the house from hell. It would be like any other household where the Sunday papers were read by everyone whilst lounging on the large bed. There were cartoons to look at and laugh about. Her father was quiet, probably sporting a sore head from an enormous hangover. Did last night really happen? Did she imagine it? The man sitting before her was not the sadistic creature who terrorised them all the night before. He appeared to be someone else.
    This continued for ten more years, as she tried desperately to deal with her parents, coping with her father's cruelty in the best way she could. She tried so hard to achieve at school. No one ever knew of her situation and consequently how she battled with low self-confidence, feelings of worthlessness and a total lack of self esteem. To this day, she has never given up and over the years has faced a great deal of adversity that has endowed her with inner strength, personal power and wisdom. She still struggles with issues involving confidence and self-esteem but through life's transitions, she has changed. Sometimes she feels almost unrecognisable in the unfamiliarity of the different life she now leads, the person she has become, but she has survived.
    If these words inspire just one person then their work is done. Thank you for accepting me into your hearts. Here is the message my story brings.

Today we see through the same eyes
She turned inwardly to see
Reflecting back out at her, love, her Self, me
She found me, I have found my Self.
You can too.

Peace by Piece

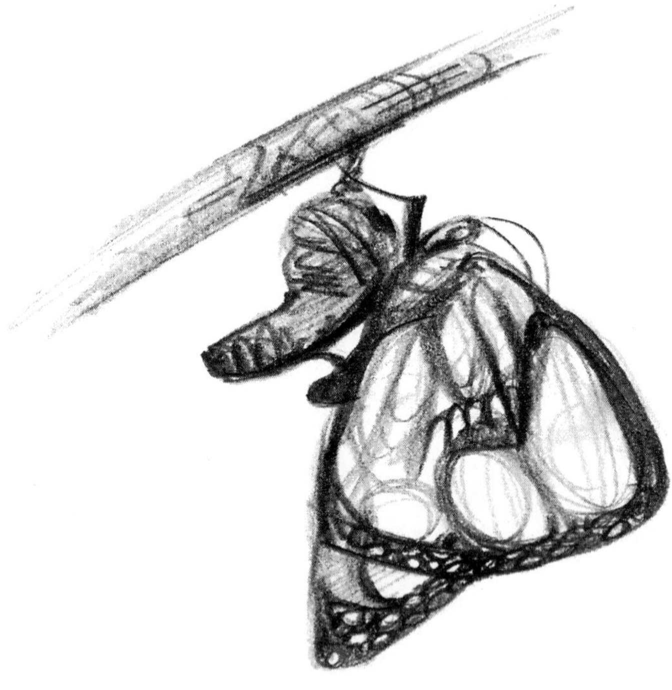

Awakening
by Nadia Stephens

Moving house again, posted to Scotland; time to uproot my 13-year-old self from life on an RAF base in Germany that had been home for 3 years. Mum frantically washed dirty hand marks from the walls, deep cleaning to erase our presence from that house. A few days before we left, at a disco, I felt peculiar, ethereal, as though part of me had already gone. Chicago sang 'about leaving and taking away a part of you, and my throat hurt like acid burns when I swallowed, I felt hot and giddy. In bed with flu I missed the last few days of school, friends came to say goodbye but Dad, missing the point entirely, sent them away because I was asleep. Goodbye was caught in my throat as I held the sweet picture of a horse they brought me as a parting gift. Its the middle of school term, nothing is complete, it's another abrupt and ragged ending.

We arrived in Scotland; I set out alone and self-reliant to explore new surroundings. I found it was a beautiful place, gently rolling farmland led to an aromatic pine forest, a dark backdrop to the silvery, sprinkled sand dunes of the nearby expansive and unpopulated beach. I followed a deserted lane, and spotted a mysterious house hidden in dense hedgerows and wondered what stories it held. The verge cascaded with verdant wild garlic, and I bent for a closer look. I flared my nostrils and inhaled the pungent scent. I relaxed to the peaceful sound of sweet spring birdsong until suddenly it's broken harshly as the screams and booms of Phantom jets coming in to land shattered it. The hedgerow ends and I find myself beside an emergency back gate to the airfield, a new place, yet a familiar sight. Elated by the sensory experience I was filled by a deep sense of my own autonomy.

Raw from letting go, I started a new school mid term;

being plunged into a new setting as an outsider shook me to the core. Break times the first few days seared my heart; I wandered around self-consciously, alone in a sea of leary teenagers, wishing I wasn't there. I tried to create a cloak of invisibility to avoid attention; I didn't like the probing questions and sneering comments in an accent that grated in my ears. They used unfamiliar words; a few times, trying to style it out, I guessed at what they meant, only realising I got it wrong as the ensuing laughter slapped me in the face. I slipped gratefully into the sanctuary of a game of catch some nice girls were playing, tame, but safe from the vulnerability and stigma of being alone.

Gradually people became familiar and I picked up the rhythm and lilt of the way they spoke, and I even found myself adopting a Scottish accent. I created an internal map of the surroundings and adapted to the different school system. In September I was transferred to the other building across town. Again with trepidation I headed into registration, the new girl in a class of students who'd known each other for years, and I braced myself as the impact of the scrutiny of strangers hit like a breaker. Not confident in my bravado, I kept my head down. Later that day we had English and to my relief I immediately clicked with the girl I sat next to. It was the difference between getting on with people you would choose, rather than people who are there. We became good friends and I was happier from finding a niche I liked.

I loved playing hockey, but not knowing anyone going I had to muster the confidence to stay on after games for hockey team practise. The team was already set up, but they needed one player at left back, and I got the position. There was a girl in the year above me at practises called Mary. One day she said some kind, friendly words to me, and it made me feel nice in a special kind of way. Butterflies fluttered in my tummy, I felt shy and probably didn't say much. After that, I became quite infatuated with her and looked out for her.

Peace by Piece

On Saturdays we played matches; one time boarding the coach I watched Mary put her bag in the overhead luggage rack, then go and sit at the back with her friends. Not having anyone to sit with I chose the seat below her bag, hoping she might come to get something out of it. Lo and behold she did. I was pretending to be asleep at the time in order to block out my awareness of sitting alone, when I heard some noise and opened my eyes to see her getting her bag. She smiled at me and said something, what I don't remember, but I was hungry for her attention and it stirred me inside like that lovely feeling of eating melting caramel ice-cream.

I can't remember what happened after that to my feelings for Mary. I think they faded due to lack of contact, and there was another girl in my class I liked from a distance later. I daydreamed about her and used the 1970's version of googling, which meant looking up her surname in the phone book and then gazing at a town map, wondering which of the two possible addresses she lived at. By my 15th birthday I felt reasonably settled at school. That year was O grade exam time, so schoolwork was intense. One particular day something different happened to break the repetitive routine of lessons; we left school in the afternoon, tasting freedom as we walked to the local theatre to watch the school play. Filing in I found myself sitting with friends somewhere near the front in the centre. The seats were red, velvety and comfortable and they gave a warm embrace. As the lights went off I relaxed in the darkness, settling down to enjoy this welcome break from schoolwork.

The play was a Midsummer Nights Dream. The girl playing the part of Puck was Lynn from hockey. We'd never spoken because she was in the year above me. She was dressed in a tightfitting black costume that revealed her slender, athletic looking body and highlighted the way she moved across the stage with agility and grace. Her naturally pretty face was framed by a short pixie style haircut, creating an androgynous look I liked. With a natural talent she embodied the mysterious, savvy and mischievous character of Puck.

Later on in the play, perhaps it was at the end, Puck came alone to the front of the stage and addressed the audience directly. I was watching intently, captivated by the way she drew the attention of the audience in a conspiratorial, seductive way. Suddenly I found she was looking at me. She's looking at me. The look is penetrating; her blue eyes twinkle like sapphires. I met her gaze and our eyes lingered, holding on. The audience ceased to exist as I became entranced and a wave of fragrant honeyed sensation rose and swept through me as if sparkling, vibrant, coloured bubbles fizzed and burst like fireworks in a dark indigo night sky, a deep resonance of whispers: awaken, awaken, awaken...

My memory ends there, though I imagine I gathered myself with surprise as the moment ended. After the play I watched out for Lynn, although I never spoke to her and didn't breathe a word of those feelings to anyone. I had no conscious interpretation of what I experienced that day; it was filed away in an unlabelled and sealed box inside me. My life continued as before. I had a boyfriend, and although he didn't make me feel like that, I liked the social status going out with him gave me, as so often girly chats with friends were about boys. I didn't realise something was missing. Exams came and finished and I left to move to England before the school year ended with another bout of flu to mark my unspoken goodbyes.

Although in those days I indulged myself daydreaming about the girls I liked, I didn't interrogate what I was doing. It was like it existed in a blind spot, a place I went to inside myself, parallel to but completely cut off from my developing identity as a teenage girl. I had no insight into what those feelings were but I must have thought I should keep them secret, as I never told anybody. It was the 1970's and lesbians were invisible, there wasn't access to information like there is now. I have no recollection of hearing the concept of lesbian mentioned in my school days, although I remember 'poofs' were denigrated. I was expected and expecting to be heterosexual, and the only vague idea I had about lesbians was that they were sad lonely people who had something wrong with them. Not an appealing option to a teenager searching for social acceptance.

Summer holidays 5 years later I lay on a hot, sun kissed grass verge with my best friend Rachael at the Severn Bridge Services. We ate a picnic while resting from hitch hiking to a festival in Cornwall. She smiled at me as we talked and suddenly the way she looked at me had a deeper meaning. Clear as the vibrant blue sky above us, at last I knew what my feelings were; she turned me on and I wanted her. It was a shared moment, we both acknowledged it without words. Over the following months I thought about nothing else. I'd fallen in love, but, still stuck in familiar habits, I kept it secret for months; I was afraid. Eventually I told her and it cost us our friendship. She was straight.

Grieving, I moved on, trying a relationship with a guy as I still told myself I wasn't a lesbian, it was just Rachael, that she was special. I was, somehow, even at that point blind to my record of liking girls since I was 6. At last, two years later, I met an out lesbian. We went for a drink and I told her my story, and then we went outside and she kissed me. Later, as we lay in bed together I had a blissful sense of coming home. From that moment I have celebrated my lesbian identity and never once regretted it. Sometimes the outside world makes it difficult but I am glad despite that and wouldn't want to change it. I was fortunate to find the lesbian feminist movement which was very strong in the 80's when I came out. It gave me both a place to be myself and a community I felt happy to belong to.

You don't have to be a certain kind of woman to be a

lesbian. We come from all walks of life and live our lives in many different ways. If you have feelings about women that you are unsure about, or that you feel you have to keep secret, there are confidential lesbian and gay helplines you can call for advice. There's also information about social groups and activities where you can meet other women, or just talk to someone safe and non-judgemental with whom you can talk to about your feelings.

Peace by Piece

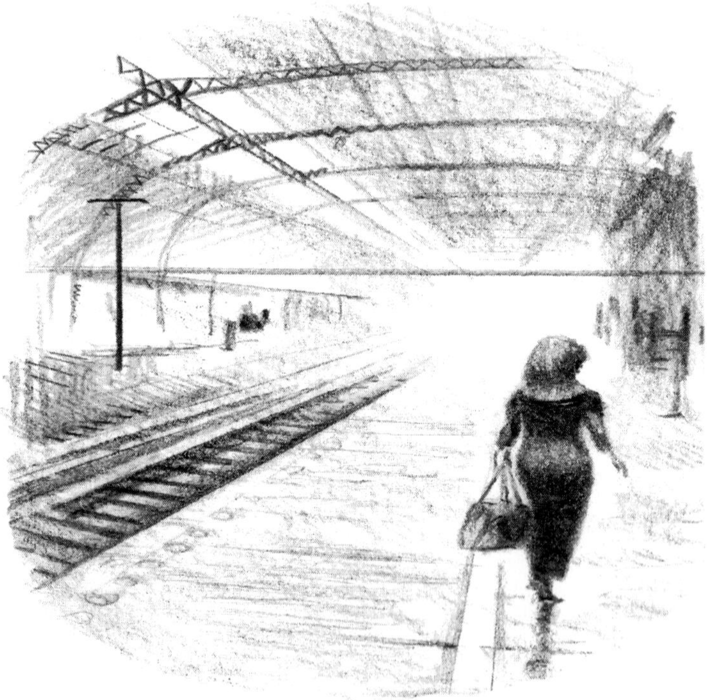

Moving On
by Anonymous

Nine years ago I arrived at Heathrow Airport from Africa and I was met by a friend. I stayed with him for two weeks, before he took me to my gran. I lived with her for more than four months, but it London it was too hard to find a job. I was in a new country, so I decided to move to South East of London.

I packed up my clothes in a suitcase and walked to the bus at London Victoria. The friend who had met me at the airport had introduced me to a friend of his, and that was where I was headed. When I reached him, I stayed there, sharing a room with other ladies whom he introduced me to as friends. I went there to look for a job, and one day I woke up and started hunting for jobs at agencies. Soon, I was lucky enough to get a job in a hospital on the weekends, and I worked there for some years.

After a while, my roommate told me she had a friend who came around sometimes, who had said he loved me. But he was too shy and it was too hard for him to tell me. I said if he can't say the words on his own, he shouldn't be sending you to say them to me. She took the message back to him.

One day we had a party, and so many people came. I can remember that day in October when he told me that he loved me, and I said to him, I have to think about it. Because the other ladies knew what was going on, and my roommate kept on pushing both sides. At the end, I went out with the man. At first we started and boyfriend and girlfriend, and at the end, it went further.

We stayed together, and at first he was okay, friendly. But after some time, the man changed. He didn't want me to talk to anybody, even to say hello. He smashed my mobile, and copied all the contacts in my phone to call and ask my

Peace by Piece

friends how they knew me, and if I was seeing other men. When I saw things were getting difficult I told him to sit down so we could talk. He told me that he was told by one friend that I was going out with other men. I asked him to tell me who it was that said that, so we can stop those things being said. He said no, and at the end, I found out he was trying to create things.

When I saw things had gotten worse, in 2007 I packed my things and went and rented a small room for £62 per week. I stayed there for three months, but there was no washing machine and it was very dirty because it was only men living in the house. We were working in the same area, and when she saw me at work he begged to see where I lived. He said he wanted to stay with me, because he needed me and he was lonely. After three months away, I went back to him and I thought maybe he had changed. But nothing had changed.

He was an alcoholic. He used to buy special brew volume nine and drink it. I'd say to him, "Why don't you stop drinking?" and he'd blame it on me, saying I'd bought it for him. He used to buy alcohol and hide it under the bin in a plastic bag. It came time to change the bin, and I lifted the bin and found it too heavy. I remember one time I found his drinks and put them all in the recycling bin. When he came back he asked if I had seen his drinks anywhere, and I told him no.

He said people had been coming to the house, that things had started disappearing. I kept quiet, and he said from now on I'm not going to hide my drinks anymore, I'll drink in the open.

In April, 2008 I got pregnant and had a hard nine months. He would kick me like a ball, telling me he wasn't the baby's father. I told him to just leave me. I have birth to my daughter, and after nine months of maternity leave, I went back to work. He stayed with the baby while I was at work.

In 2010 I got pregnant a second time. It was the same

Peace by Piece

situation throughout. I remember I went to the hospital in pain at 2:00pm and left my daughter with my friend. He was working the night shift, and he never bothered to call the hospital to find out if I was okay. I'd told him before he left that I wasn't well. When he got back to the house that morning and no one was there, he called and said where are you? I said I'm at home, I gave birth to a boy. I took another nine months maternity leave, and then went back to work. He stayed home with the kids on the weekends while I was working.

We were living in a private house, and the rent was £1000 per month, without council tax, and we had to share the rent. He told me that he would pay £800, and I would pay £200 and other expenditures and bills. But he didn't calculate how much it would be, plus the home shopping. That's when the arguing started, because he didn't want to pay the full rent, and I had to do all the rest.

In 2012, he came back from a party drunk. I had been at the party, and heard the speaker than him because he had bought all the drinks for people until the party was finished. I told him he didn't want to spend his money on the house, but he could spend it on someone's party. He said, "okay, let's account how much you are getting: you're working, you get tax credit, working tax, child benefits, and you even get support to pay the rent. Don't you know how much I spend on nappies and everything?"

One time he came home and the door was locked, but he had his own key. Instead of opening the door he kicked it open. He came upstairs, it was 23:00, and asked why the door was locked. I said it was always locked, and he had a key. He answered with a slap. It annoyed me and I told him it was the last time he would do that. If he did it again I would call the police. I was tired of being treated like a slave. He came at me, told me to call the police. I picked my phone up and called, and ran out of the house. The police didn't come,

39

though, because I called while I was running and didn't give them the address.

The next day he came back with his brother and they started packing their things, whatever they needed, and he went and stayed with his friends. He was happy, saying he was free and was no longer a baby sitter. But after a month things changed. He started texting, emailing and sending his friends to talk to me. He wanted to sit and talk. So on 14th December 2012, his friend arranged for us to meet on a Sunday and talk with his mum there. I accepted, and said I would go and hear his side, because he was telling people that I chased him out of the house.

So, I went. He called two elderly people, his mum and two close friends. But I went on my own, with nobody there to support me. He started to talk first and he said things he doesn't want me to do. After I answered him, after the discussion was finished, I told him I don't need you calling me a prostitute in front of the kids and your family. It doesn't make sense to say with you if you have no trust or faith.

When he left he had the spare key to the house. He would come over sometimes and pick up his letters, including mine. I spent a month without getting any mail until I was told by the house share mates that he kept coming to get the mail. I decided to move, and I found a house because I was frustrated. I moved away so he wouldn't know where I was, but kept working in the same place.

I was at work at lunch one day with my colleagues, sharing the time he came over my back without knowing, I heard when he stood at the back and said, I have been watching you people all the time with my wife, but be careful. He slapped me and walked out of the hospital. I shouted and the supervisor came. They called security and they ran after him. He was caught. I don't know what he told them because they didn't even bother to call me to hear my side, but I thought they left and said it was just a problem between a husband and a wife.

One day I came home from shopping and I went to the bus stop. I saw him walking towards me. He said he wanted to give me things for the kids, but he was a person who never wanted to spend a coin buying even a sweet. I told him to take it to them himself.

My life was getting too hard, I was stressed all the time. I had stopped working, and moved to be near my friends. My kids couldn't go to school, and my daughter was scared. She was afraid he was going to kill me. I asked myself what I was doing, living this threatened life. I checked online and got a number for domestic abuse and asked them what help they could give. They said, Are you safe to talk now? I said I was. I spoke to them and they asked me if I wanted to settle someone or any other kind of help. I started packing, and after packing I called a cab to move me to Nottingham.

I stayed in a refugee place (which I don't want to name) for six months, then I applied for homeless assistance. It didn't take long, and I got a house in Nottingham. I moved to the area without knowing anybody, and there was no one to talk to and they weren't my friends. After some time, things settled down. I don't have friends, but I'm okay. I'm free, and rebuilding my life. The man is no longer in my life, and my kids are happy and going to school, something they weren't able to do when we were moving so often.

Being a woman on your own in a new country is hard. Making a decision to leave a man who is abusing you is hard. But if you look for people who can help you, if you are open about what you need and honest about where your life is, then you can get to a better place. You can be strong, you have to be. Things are harder for women. You have to move forward. You have to start a new life for yourself, not for anyone else. I'm starting my new life; seeing my kids happy, and being happy myself.

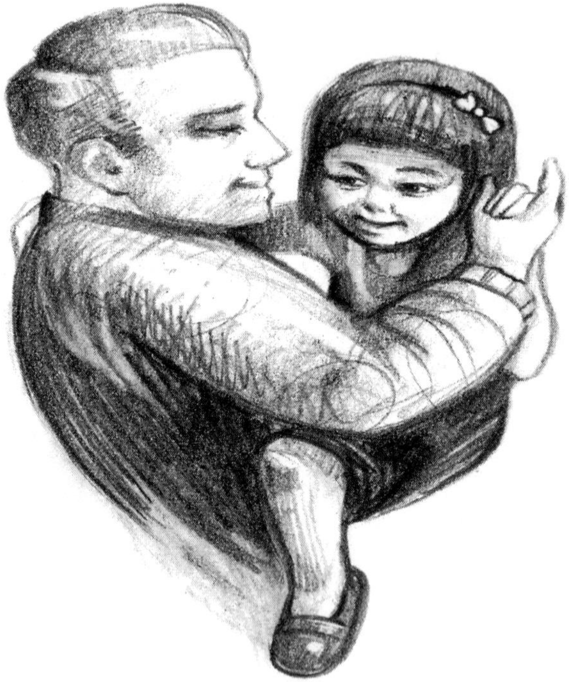

The Daughter. The Death. The Danger.
by Katie Gallagher

All growth is preceded by death. My own was no different. I learnt that the Spring's redemption was born out of the cold corpse of winter. I did not expect to see the green shoots of revelation and understanding in the desolate wasteland of grief that I inhabited after my father's death, and yet, that's exactly where they were.

The year preceding his death had been hard for both of us. The weight of time and illness had crushed the vitality and power and confidence from him. In its wake was left a vulnerable, frightened, and miserable old man.

I had played the diligent, dutiful daughter my whole life. I knew his aggressive orders to warm his porridge were to hide his fear and anxiety, yet as he hobbled from his bed to the bathroom, I felt a lethal cocktail of rage and resentment brewing inside me. How dare he demand so much compassion from me, when he had shown so little towards my mother? I felt angry, spiteful, vindictive. Tears stung my eyes and as they fell I stirred them into his porridge, stirred in sorrows for my sick, saintly mother, who was martyred long ago on the cross of marriage and motherhood.

He did visit her, I grant him that. He would sit by her hospital bed. He went dutifully every evening. He always kissed her perfunctorily on the cheek, he asked how she was, and paid little attention to what she said. He sat moodily in the chair saying nothing, night after night, for over a year. Sometimes he fell asleep and she would wake him when it was time to go.

She told me how they had met in The Palais all those years ago. Back then, she was a nurse, tall and slim and lovely, out with Bridie and Kate for the dancing on a Saturday night. She recalled how handsome he was in his smart suit and his crop of lovely curls. He was with my Uncles, John Joe and Jimmy, out for the craic. She said he swaggered over and asked her to dance. He was an incredible dancer, waltzing, foxtrot, quick step. You name it, she said, he could dance it. Apparently no couple could hold a candle to them on the dance floor. She was in heaven in his arms, lost in the rhythm of the music. The courtship was turbulent, but after a few pints and a few dances the rows were forgotten. In their wedding photos, I could see their beauty and their faces lit up with hope and expectation.

She told me often of their many blessings. Four of us healthy children and all his hard work paid off with a lovely house in a nice neighbourhood, and a profitable business, but I saw the bankrupt marriage. Looking back, I can see their emotional bank accounts were constantly overdrawn. He drank too much, sulked too much, worked too much, shouted and ranted too much. She cried too much, mothered too much, kept quite too much, carried the can too much. So slowly over the years, the rows and recriminations were replaced by illness and silence.

I did see some tenderness seep out now and then, when he held her hand briefly as she lay in her white hospital bed. But then death came and saved her from those silences and left him to grieve for that lovely girl he had swept across the dance floor.

And so concealed beneath the satin cloak of kindness and concern in which I visited him and tended to his medical needs, I wore a thick black corset of bitterness and blame. It grew tighter and tighter over the years whenever he barked his orders at me, or lodged his incessant complaints or failed to show a shred of the gratitude I so desperately desired.

I didn't give up. I came dutifully every day. I kissed him perfunctorily on the cheek and asked him how he was, but paid little attention to what he said. Then death came and saved me from those silences and left me to grieve for that handsome haunted father who had, long ago, swept me across the kitchen dance floor in my red velvet dress. I felt strangely liberated, and yet... So lost. So lonely. But I couldn't weep, the corset wouldn't weaken. So much unsaid. Regrets, though, cannot raise the dead.

Then I found that brown crumpled package in the bottom of his wardrobe. It was tied up with dressing gown rope into an incongruously neat bow. Decades of dust had deleted it from earlier detection. I folded open the thick waxy paper. My hands were shaking as I fumbled through the ancient photographs, which he had so tenderly preserved of his beloved Rose at the dance where he had proposed. He had kept the receipts for her wedding and engagement rings and their modest wedding breakfast with just fifteen guests, most of whom are long gone.

Longing flooded through me as I saw the letter from my mother. It was penned in her beautiful copper plate handwriting in her own intimate style, which had always comforted and consoled me whenever I received the blue Basildon Bond envelope and saw my name in her flowery hand. "My Darling Michael," it began. This was such an ordinary letter about her night shifts in the hospital, her domestic duties and her excitement at seeing him again at the dance on Saturday. It broke my heart. I wept and wept for what might have been and never was. Their love was crushed like heather under the heavy boots my father wore to protect and defend himself.

During that year before his death, I had sat with him night after night, desperate to lift his misery and melancholy, eager to please him with my questions about his life. He never betrayed any pleasure in my interest; he seemed too consumed by the bitterness of his past and the fear of no future. He spat out the horrors of his early life at school with such venom it frightened me. He still hated that sadistic schoolmaster who had taken such satisfaction in the daily beatings with a rod which left his body black and blue and left his emotions damaged and retarded for the rest of his life. "They ruled us", he growled, "those priests and teachers. We had no say. We were treated like animals, no, worse than animals, you wouldn't beat an animal like that every single day. Yet still," he said, we had to go." At home there was little time for kindness, either. There were eight mouths to feed off a few acres of bogland. There were jobs to do before school and jobs to do after school. Water to draw from the well, cows to herd home for milking, hay to turn and dry and harvest. Plenty of them in the bed. Plenty of them around the table. Plenty never said.

His memory had drawn a veil of sentimentality over the poverty at home, but my questions brought up that bitter bile from school. Time and frailty and old age had not withered his rage at those bastards who had so cruelly tortured that little boy so long ago.

During that poignant period between his death and burial when planning his funeral, polishing his eulogy and poking through his belongings, I discovered the sacred gifts of revelation and understanding. That afternoon when I was alone with him in the funeral home, as he lay there silently in his satin coffin, my own resentment towards that unemotional, ungrateful father melted into compassion. I wept with empathy and agony for that damaged little boy who had then damaged his little girl with his vicious, volatile temper which erupted without warning. She had lived in a state of vigilance and fear, ever watchful for the next vomit of vulgar, violent abuse or the terrifying chaos of broken china or broken chairs.

At last I could contextualize his constant criticisms, or his fist thumping episodes when I struggled to understand an instruction which triggered his rambling rants of how thick I was, so much thicker than the wall under his fist. There was a realization of why he greeted my mistakes with vindictive glee, which cut deeper than the shame of the original sin, whatever it was. That rage against the cruelty of his teacher was vented on me, in ignorance and unawareness.

His death and illness proved to be my redemption. The knowing and forgiving had saved me from the danger of wearing that black corset to my own grave. So as we lowered his coffin into that cold clay, I buried with him all that toxic rage which had insidiously constricted my soul for all those years.

This parable of pain was written to heal and to help.

Hurt people, hurt people. They don't mean to, but they do. Only you can break the chain. Your parents are guilty of whatever they did to you, but not to blame. You are an adult now, do not do, as I did, for too long, and feel and think like a child. Seek to understand. Feel your rage, vent it, then heal your pain. Learn to love yourself. You cannot change the past. You cannot love your children more than you can love yourself. For your sake, and for theirs, let it go.

I wish you well.

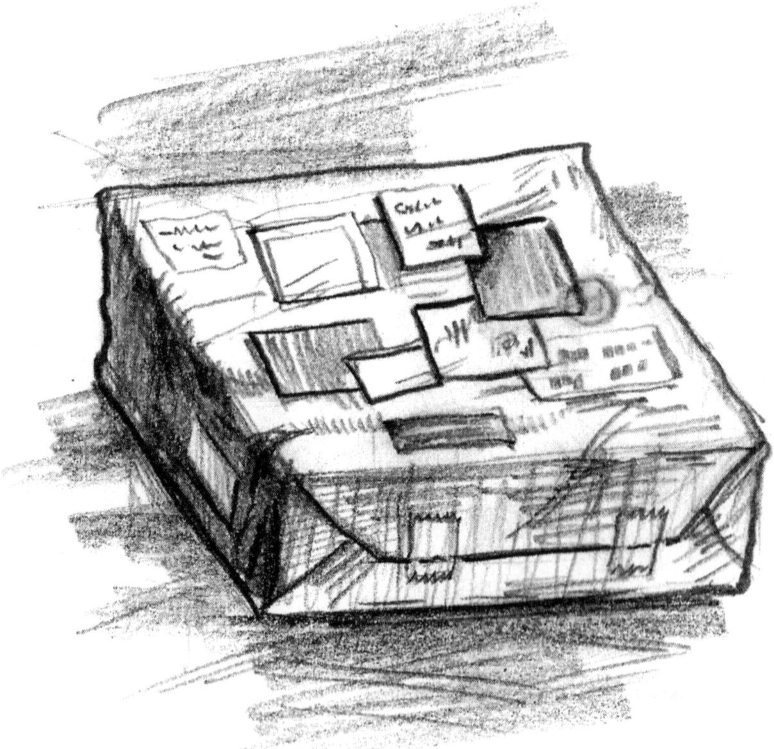

Labelled
by A.Woman

In the distance, the cloaked hooded figure was just visible,. a grey apparition that seemed neither solid nor transparent, but like something in between. It appeared to be either floating or hovering over the ground. It was hard to tell from a distance and my mind struggled to give the shape form. An ashen mist spiralled and surrounded the creature. This added further confusion and I could only just make out the line of some 'thing' that resembled a human form. The apparition continued to tease my mind, fading and shape shifting and never really solidifying into whatever it was meant to be.

The surrounding landscape was reminiscent of plush green hill tops with vibrant velvet valleys. They were interspersed with meandering, shining silver streams that flashed with star light. The sky was pink-blue as if just before the dawn of a beautiful day, full of promise and new beginnings. In contrast, the shadowy figure was vague and dirty. It moved around as if to hide but it couldn't hide its cloudy and murky form anywhere. Then, when my mind focussed on the creature for a second it started to reveal its true identity, but only in patches. Parts of it were taking form, then vanishing and becoming distant.

Then, all of a sudden, it solidified into its true shape.

I awoke from the dream confused and dazed, gasping for breath. I was soaked through with sweat and my bed clothes and pyjamas where wrapped around me like cold wet rope. I felt restricted and suffocated by the damp fabric and it felt like I had been bound and tied like a corpse. Using my arms and legs I fought for a time, trying to break free of the items, then I rested from my soggy battle for a few minutes to consider. I felt my mind and body become anxious and panicked as the details of the dream filtered through once more. I lay there wondering what it all meant. Surely something as grim as that would have a message or meaning. I went and changed into something dry and the relief of that was good. My partner entered the bedroom with breakfast balanced on trays, boiled eggs, coffee and fresh orange juice. A normal breakfast for a normal morning, but I felt abnormal and disturbed by the vision of the dream from the night before. I started to recount what I had dreamt about to him and he sat poised with his tray on his lap, ready to listen. As I started to talk his eyebrows and forehead crinkled as he tried to absorb what I was saying.

It dawned on me as I was recounting the dream that the figure I had seen resembled the grim reaper. I felt a cold shiver run down my spine as I saw the image clearer in my mind's eye. This time it was apparent to me that as I stared at the grim spectre, it was staring right back at me. A further shiver took hold of my body and graduated into a full shudder which affected my voice as I spoke. I asked my partner, "Do you think this means anything?" He just sat there, speechless, with a concerned look on his face and shrugged his shoulders. As the most consistent person in my life at that time his opinion was important to me, and I felt even he was at a loss to advise me. I did feel slightly better for disclosing the details of the dream to him but I couldn't stop a further cold shiver prick through me until I was actually shaking with the fear and morbid apprehension you get when something bad is coming your way.

As I sat there in bed I realised I couldn't carry on like this anymore, as I felt like I had reached the end. Of what? I didn't know. It just felt like The End and I didn't want to explore what that actually meant. All I knew was that the dream had left me feeling cold, sick and uncertain when I had woken up. I am a mature, middle aged woman who has had more than her fair share of experience, so why would I be dreaming of things like this? It all felt like it was serious, very serious, like life and death serious, my life and death serious. My mind raced as I tried to make sense of it all, but how could I? I struggled further to give it some interpretation different to what I thought it might actually mean, as it all scared me witless and I didn't want to die. Then I remembered what I had been voicing to my partner recently at home. Basically, I had been discussing with him what the point of my existence was. What was the point of me being on this planet? Did my life have a purpose? I ruminated over these statements for a short time, then I started to think about it all, I mean really think about what it all meant.

As I lay there in bed pondering all the possible meanings of the dream and the feelings it had evoked in me, I realised I am me and there is no one else like me. I wasn't saying I'm a special, unique, great individual or anything like that. But I am just me. Just your common garden variety peri-menopausual, empty nester, anxious, dizzy, female human being and that was all right with me. I sighed, my breath rushed out of my mouth in a huff and my shoulders sank low. I asked my partner if he was all right with me too. He just sighed, nodded, shrugged his shoulders and smiled too. I thought even more deeply and arrived at the following conclusion: We all live in a world where it is becoming more increasingly important to feel you need to be or do something in order to define yourself as who you are. Where the pressure is on to constantly give yourself a label in order to fit in with society. It doesn't matter if it is a positive or negative label.

Sometimes people really like to use the negative ones on you, as it really makes their day to carry on degrading and belittling you to the point where you're left scraping yourself off the floor. Their label needs to define you in some way, as society doesn't feel comfortable unless it knows what you are, what you do and more specifically, where you fit in within that society, either positively or negatively. Negative labels are preferred by your haters, abusers and users, which isn't surprising really, but labels of all sorts can be given to you. For example: beautiful or mentally ill, compassionate or disabled, criminal or artistic. I have, during my lifetime, been given all sorts of labels by people, including by those who were unexpected, including family members, friends, work colleagues, partners and lovers. You don't realise how many labels people have forced onto you until you start to think about it and how many rotten, dysfunctional people who only wish to ridicule and hurt you have labelled you in order to do so. Some I have been guilty of giving to myself, but mostly they have been given by the aforementioned.

The fact is, once you have a label, you're then supposed to live up to it. If you are unable to, then this can result in your death. The spectre of the grim reaper floated about in front of my eyes, reminding me of that assumption. Was it true? I stiffened slightly, remembering my thought processing after my dream. As I already said, virtually everyone I have come across has decided to label me in some way. I have been known as a single parent without prospects, a career failure, partially sighted or monocular visioned, mentally unstable, financially stupid, anxiety ridden, dysfunctional, an easy rape victim, a domestic abuse attractor, a family of origin breaker-upper, addicted, needing psychological help, sexually confused, emotionally stunted, ugly, flat chested, a sexual abuse deserver, and even 'you will end up schizo like your mum.' Lovely how people can communicate with you, is it not? And these are just some of the more positive ones. As you can see, I have a sense of humour too.

With all these labels, and others, firmly attached to my person by the label deliverers, I strove to prove them all wrong. All these labels did was make me feel ill and that my life wasn't worth living. Hence the dream, perhaps?

I just couldn't keep up with the struggle these labels evoked any more. They only reinforced the labellers ideas if

Peace by Piece

I tried to change people's minds and opinions of me. I didn't want to continue with the fight any more, as it felt like that had started to happen a long time ago when these labels were first given to me. The noise and the pain in my head was unbearable I felt sick and on edge with it all. No wonder I was constantly worried and stressed. I felt frozen to the spot and my mind started to scream even louder... who am I? WHO AM I?

As I tried to think of the answer to that question I started to get angry at the labellers who thought they had the right to describe who I am. My head was pounding with the rushing pressure of blood coursing through my temples. The anger was rising like hot red bile from the furnace of my stomach and I blinked back tears of hatred towards these people. When I had calmed down later I simply said to myself, you are lovely, strong, and kind, you are courageous, empathetic and bright. You are ALL of the best labels in the world and more. You are fine. As I lay there in bed I realised I had to give up these labels, everyone else's labels. They were toxic now, dangerous and poisonous, harmful and soul destroying. I knew it wasn't going to be easy, as I had been conditioned so well to describe myself by my given labels. They had become part of me, but I decided it was now life and death, MY life and death, and I had to choose. So I started to choose life.

I think what I was really trying to say to myself and to anyone else this concerns, is that you don't need a label. There doesn't need to be a point to your existence, just because someone else thinks there should be. You are fine as you are. It should be up to you, and you alone, if you want to create a label or have a point to your life. No one else has the right to determine or define who you are by labelling you. My head was starting to clear. I felt lighter and happier and more at peace. I stretched out in bed and allowed a smile to myself. It felt like the horizon on the landscape of my life was starting to be free and clear of the spectre that had once presided there. I got out of bed, opened the curtains and started to get on with the rest of my life.

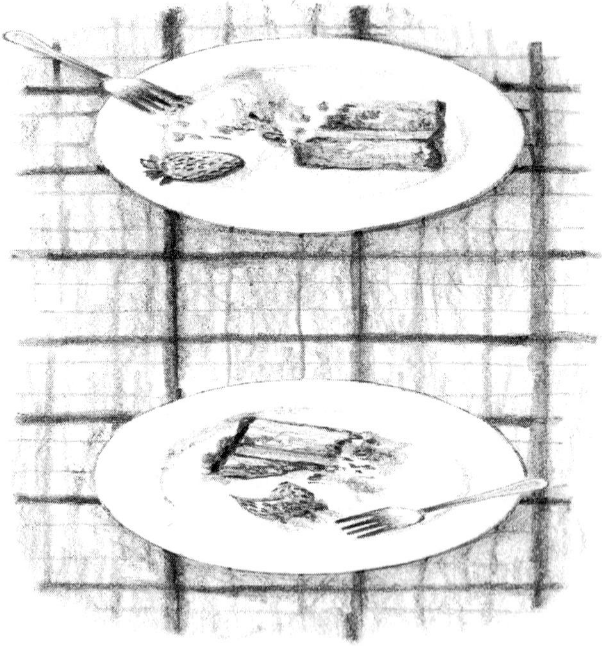

JOSEY
By Alex Mawson-Harris

1

I was going to tell you about the most difficult time in my life, when I was a teenager being a dick and alienating my family and friends, and how far I've come since then. But walking through the fields near to my house, the winter sun shining lovely and bright, I realised that I could instead further improve myself. I could fall in love again.

I decided to call my lover-turned-friend:

"Hello Darling...Thank you for calling me back. I'm good thank you...good...Darling, I love you. I think we should work on ourselves... I think we've let ourselves go, and that we should make things good again and fall back in love..."

2

As I headed towards the Derby train station, my underfoot crunching in the compact snow, I felt a cool sense of relaxation: it was the weekend. Once inside, I searched the electronic board for the Nottingham train— the next wasn't for another fifteen minutes. I decided to make good use of the time, and so took the few steps to the Costa Coffee. I mulled over my options and proceeded to talk with the barista. I asked for a gingerbread latte without the latte, half expecting a quizzical look. To my delight, he smiled and remarked that he also had this drink, making me feel welcome. After paying for my beverage, I left Costa Coffee to board the Nottingham train.

Months later, as I headed towards the Derby train station once again, there was a warm edge of sunshine bouncing off the car windows; spring was in full bloom. I quickly glanced at the time board, before trying to come up with a drink to order. Full of hope, I finally met eyes with the same barista I had been served by a few months previous.

"You're wearing glasses today," I noted in a cheery tone. He smiled in agreement before telling me that he only wore contacts some of the time. After a little more chitchat, I ordered a hot chocolate with cream and marshmallows so as to blend in as a customer, before giving myself away through meaningless questions about meaningless loyalty cards.

Once seated at the edge of the room, fixed between the large glass doors and the counter, I nursed the hot chocolate nervously. I felt slightly surprised, and quite awkward, when the famous barista started rearranging the magazine rack, located within my sphere of personal space.

A delighted smile pulled at the corners of my mouth as I subtly slipped the piece of paper he had cleverly placed onto my table into my pocket. From that moment, every minute was a blushing hour of excitement and angst. I made it through five heart-pounding minute-hours before smiling and saying goodbye.

I wore a grin that was utterly infectious. Whilst waiting on the train platform, a passer by gave me a flirtatious smile, and I felt that today was, for me, a lucky one.

After sitting down on the train, I read the piece of paper:
Josey
07791468640
I sent him a message. "Hi Josey, your handwriting is beautiful..."

3

Our first date was lovely. He showed me around the exhibitions of a photography festival and we had a go at making some pinhole photographs. When the lights turned off, he took my hand and electricity sparked through us. We became best friends while waiting for two old men to get off a train simulator who were talking about acid and the revolution. Subsequent dates were nice also, relaxing in the sun, his Aerobe Frisbee around his neck making him a tombola prize, countless cinema trips, and the time we ordered all the deserts on the menu.

Four years later, in retrospect, with all of our ups and downs, the good and the bad times, we have been pretty solid. We've been there for one another, and have shared a lot of love.

Hitting a rock, a stale mate and letting ourselves go, growing distant and sometimes even cold, we have felt like giving up. That it's only a matter of time before we move on with our lives, leaving our love behind. But I've realised that that isn't our only option. We could improve things, regain our strength, and if love doesn't blossom, we can float away as our best selves, as best friends, and on a high.

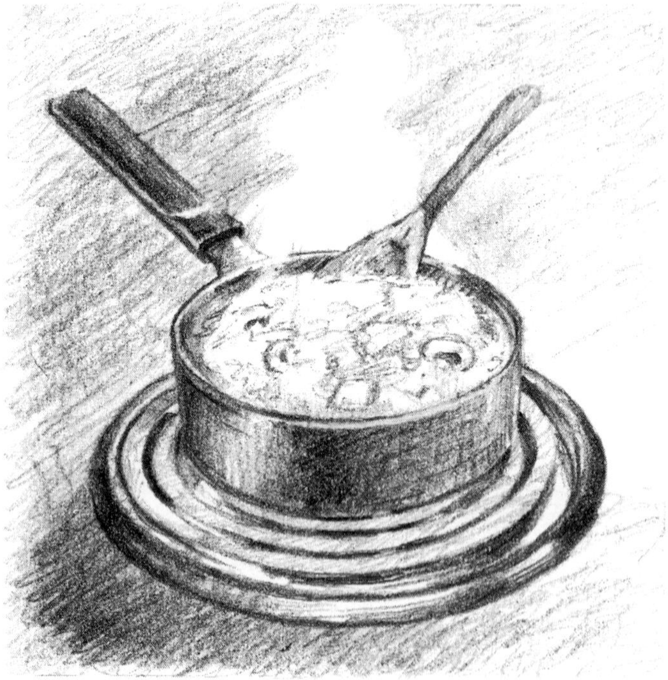

Differences
by Aisha

My name is Aisha and I'm from Sudan. I live here with my family, my husband and my two sons. We came here together seven years ago. I love my family, they are my life. I also love cooking. In the future, I would like to go back to my country, if the government gets better, because the rest of my family is there, and I miss them too.

There are many differences between my country and the UK. For example, the weather is Sudan is not like the weather in the UK. In Sudan it is very hot in the summer, but in the UK, the weather is not good, even in the summer. Every day it is cold and raining. The food in my country is really delicious, but the favourite food in the UK is just fish and chips. But the people in the UK are very good. In my country people are also very friendly.

I like the UK because I have a good life here. I like England because the government helps people in any way. My husband has kidney problems, and must have dialysis three times a week for an hour each time. In Sudan, he would not get the care he needs because he would have to pay for it there, and it is far too expensive. The medicine here is free, but in Sudan, it is not.

Here, my son studies at University, but he could not do that there.

Sudan used to be good, but problems in the government have made it bad. That's why we came to the UK—for a better life. I go back to Sudan to visit my family every two years. I get to visit my sister and my friends, but many of my brothers have moved. I have eight brothers, spread out around the world, in Sudan, America, Spain and Egypt. They all left Sudan because of the government.

I enjoy my time in Sudan, but I'm always happy to come back to my life here in the UK too.

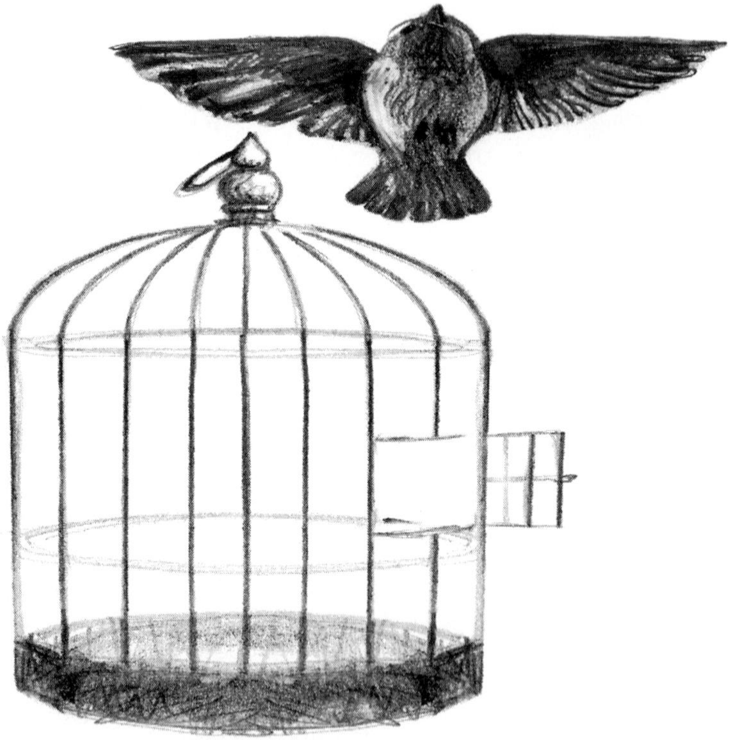

A NEW LIFE
by Anonymous

In my country, you must go into military service for two years when you become eighteen years old. In 1998, I was eighteen, it was my turn to go into the military. At the time, I was very happy inside. I met a lot of people who spoke other languages, ate other traditional foods and saw the way other people dressed and communicated. I met more people who worked in logistics and the arsenal, and we had so much fun joking and laughing, and I liked that. It was a good time, and then I went back to my home for a while.

After six months, in June 2000 I went back into the military. The Eritrean war started with Ethiopia in June, a massive war about the border. I was working first aid, to help people fighting in the war. It was very hard work, day and night, without breaks. Work. No break. Work. No food. Work. No break. It was too dark, and there was no light available. It was like that for three months, and it got worse and worse. It was a very hard time, a very bad time. When the war ended it was too far away from my home. I ended up hiding in a mud hut, 300 meters away from the military base. I took a bus to my home, because I couldn't stay in the military anymore, it was too much for me.

My father and my mother said, "You have to go back. Please, go back to Masawa!"

I said, "No."

"Please, go!"

"No!"

In January the soldiers came to my home, and took me back to the military compound, and I was not happy. I was angry because of the shock of so many soldiers' deaths. I was very scared, and everything, day and night, was dark for me.

After one year, in 2002, I was better. Everything with the people around me was good, with lots of communication and good relationships.

I continued working in first aid because I liked helping people. I was happy with that work. In 2004 while in military service I met a boy friend. We had a good time. I liked him, and he even liked me! We worked together, and I was so happy.

In 2006 we married—his name was Simon. It was nice, the military gave us a month holiday. We enjoyed our time off, and then we both headed back out to our military posts. But we were in different places, and because we weren't together, it was very hard for me. Different places, and then different countries. I couldn't stay with my husband, and his life had also changed. Everything I liked about this life had changed.

Then, a year later, I was sent to prison. I was caught praying at a friend's house while I was on holiday from the military, and soldiers are not allowed to pray outside their own homes. The government does not like my religion, either. And so my husband and I were both in prison for four months. It was so hard for us. After four months in prison, at night time, 2:00am, I was hiding because there was a storm, with terrible strong winds. Everybody has got chains on, and suddenly the door is broken by the wind. Then I was out with two other people, running. Seven of us got out that night. After a long time walking, we found a small village. I knew a lady there, someone I had known a long time. She hid us in her house and gave us food, and allowed us to have a shower. We stayed with her for two days, and then we started away again with a "business man." She made an agreement with him, that he would take us to Sudan. But he was a bad man.

When he took us to his home, we didn't know how to speak Arabic, we didn't know anything that was going on. The place, the culture, the language—everything was too difficult for us. After three months, the man processed my paperwork, and I could leave. But my friend Sarah stayed with him, because she didn't have the money to pay for her paperwork. I was not happy, I was scared. He was a criminal, and he treated people like slaves. If they couldn't pay, then they were forced to stay with him and do things for him. They weren't allowed to pray or to read the Bible. I didn't want to leave Sarah with him, but I had no choice.

I entered the UK with another "business man," one who lived in the UK. After one day in the UK I applied to become an asylum seeker. I told them about prison in our country, and how we were persecuted and put in prison. The immigration people were sad for me. They gave me paperwork that says I can stay for five years, and when I got that, I could bring my husband over to be with me. We lived together around three years, but he changed.

His behaviour changed. He drank and went out, day and night. I became very unhappy, very sad, and we separated.

I met a new boyfriend, and I've got a daughter with him. I enjoy time with my daughter, and with my boyfriend, but I've never forgotten my friend Sarah. She is living in another country, and she is still not settled. Before I got pregnant, I was working full time job. After I had my daughter, I stopped working. I was helping Sarah, sending her money when I could, and calling her so she didn't feel so lonely, but now I can't help her, it's too difficult. If I worked, I could change her life. And I want to, because she is a nice person. She is everything for me, like a sister. I've known her for more than fifteen years. I remember all these things in the past, things that were very hard, very bad. And I will remember Sara for the rest of my life.

I miss my family, and I miss my home. I go back sometimes to visit, and when I come back to the UK I miss the big family gathering together. But mostly, I'm happy here. I go to church, I pray, and I don't have to worry about going to prison for it. And I don't have to worry about my daughter going through what I did.

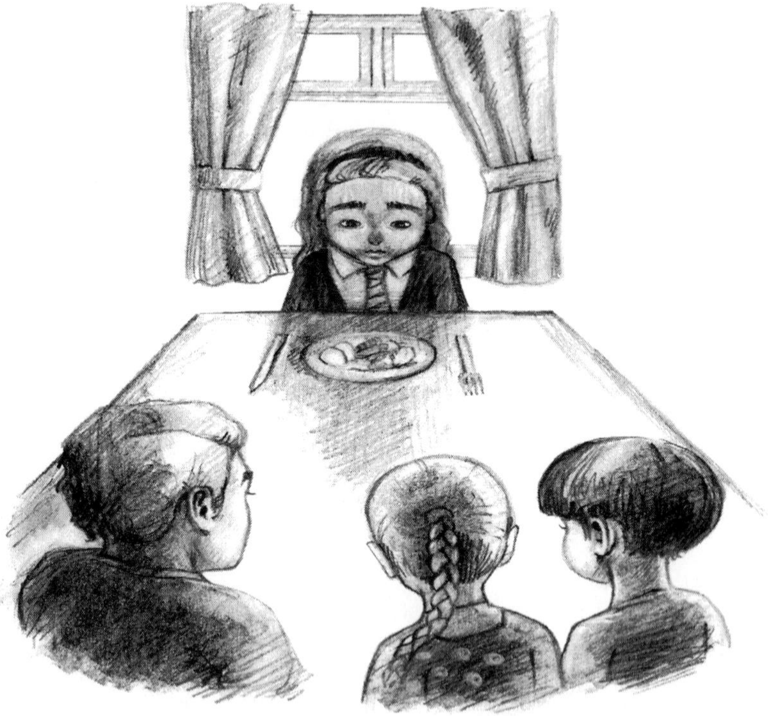

You'll Turn Into a Chip
By Iona Tamburrino

I don't like school. I'm different to the other children. No one likes me. Thank goodness I'm home. I'm sitting here alone on our lovely enormous corner sofa with orange and brown spots on it. I like how when I caress the fabric of the spots the fabric changes from matt to shiny beneath my finger. Is dinner-time over yet? I can hear my family in the dining room talking and laughing and enjoying their disgusting dinner. I look down at my plate. Spaghetti with tomato sauce. Or is it? It smells different to normal. Has mum blended carrots in the sauce again? Or has she spooned sauce out of the bolognaise? I check for tiny meaty bits. There's one! I am not eating this! I'm so hungry. Why did mum spoil my dinner? She knows I only like plain tomato sauce. I pick up the fork from the plain brown coffee table and try to make it look like I've eaten a bit. Right, how am I going to do this? I can't hide spaghetti! I can't flush any down the loo because they'll hear me. I start to move the spaghetti around the flowery plate, trying to pile more on one side.

"Are you going to play with your food or are you going to eat it?" Mum says.

How long has she been standing there? She looks tired, pretty, but tired, with her apron on and her long brown hippy hair. I can't wait for dinner to be over so I can go to my room and be by myself.

"I'm not hungry." I lied.

Mum sighed and took my plate. My younger brother and sister came bounding into the room, racing for the TV remote. I go to my room but I can still smell it. It makes me feel sick. I try to think of other smells. Books smell nice. I pick up my Ladybird copy of Snow White & the Seven Dwarves and pretend I can't smell that yucky smell anymore. I hate it. It's disgusting. It's meat.

Peace by Piece

This had become a regular thing, me eating in the lounge. I had started to spoil dinner-time for everyone else. I didn't mean to. The smell of meat on everyone else's plates would make me heave. But it wasn't just the smell that made meal times difficult. I know my parents love me. They're so very loving. My dad would sit me on his knee and call me his "skinny rabbit". I didn't think anything of it. I didn't know what skinny was or what fat was. I just liked the idea of being called a rabbit. I loved rabbits. They were so cute. I hoped dad would get me one, one day. But dinner-times. Dinner-times I just wanted to disappear.

Sitting at the dining table with my family would always start with excitement as everyone would hungrily race to the table. We would all pause while Mum or Dad said grace. My brother and sister would open an eye, look at one another and then look at me. We would all giggle. It's always hard not to when you're not supposed to. Then there'd be chatter and laughter while everyone ate ravenously and discussed their day. I'd join in with the chatter too. Then suddenly, someone would notice I wasn't eating. I heard their voices but I was so ashamed I couldn't look up to see who was speaking.

"Come on love, you have to eat something."
"Mmm, it's really nice. Yummy."
"What don't you like about it?"
"You used to love this!"
"Is everything okay at school?"
"Look it's carrots, darling. You like carrots."

Not today I don't. I thought to myself, wishing everyone would shut up and let me attempt it myself in my own time.

"Just try a little bit."
"Just try it!"
"Just eat something!"

The table would fall silent as yet again with everyone's attention on me, I could feel my cheeks burn while everyone

Peace by Piece

stared. They were all eating slowly now, watching me. Waiting for me to eat like a normal person. My cheeks flared and I had goose-bumps all over. A metallic taste in my mouth. I could feel tears starting to fall, so much so that I could barely see my plate anymore.

Please don't force me. I begged internally. I don't know why, but I felt afraid. Bullied, even. But I knew they cared and only wanted me to be like them so I could be happy and healthy.

"I'll have your carrots if you don't want them. You can have my roastie if you want?" said my sister, trying to help.

I loved her for it. And my brother, bless him, would be trying to change the subject. I knew he was trying to take the attention off me. Even my littlest sister in her highchair ate better than me. I couldn't even take my vitamin and iron tablets in front of anyone because they were so big they'd make me choke.

Why was I so fussy with food? Why did I hate meat so much? I remember aged six, when children at school told me in the playground that sausages are pig's willies. I believed them. I also remember, around the same time, school lunch. I was queuing up with my tray in my gingham summer dress and cardigan. There was no choice of what was for dinner. The dinner-lady behind the serving counter put the lumpy mashed potatoes on my plate with an ice cream scoop. I saw the meat balls swimming in gravy.

"Please can I not have the meat?" I asked her shyly, quietly and with complete embarrassment at my being difficult.

"You get the same as everyone else. It's good for you. A healthy balanced meal. Potatoes, mixed vegetables and meat!" She barked back as if I were wasting her time.

At the table I picked out the peas to eat. The mashed potatoes were spoiled because they were drenched in meat juice. The dinner-lady came over and crouched down to my

Peace by Piece

level.

"Are you going to try the meatballs?" She said in a kind voice, which I didn't trust after she had snapped at me earlier.

"I don't like meat," I said.

"You have to eat them."

"I don't want to."

"You're going to eat them!" She picked up a meat ball with her hand, opened my mouth with her other one and forced it to the back of my mouth. I choked and gagged and cried. Oddly, the only taste I noticed was that of her fingers. The other children stared at the scene I'd caused and I spent the remainder of lunch-time crying into my plate.

I fainted once at school. From hunger. I was ill all the time. Tonsillitis, the flu...It seemed I needed time off sick every month. I remember pretending to dinner ladies that I had been off sick when I hadn't so that I could eat at different table. Otherwise you always had to sit at the same table. And I was always sat with people I didn't know or bullies who'd stare and make fun of me. I was never sat with anyone I would feel comfortable eating in front of

Hooray it's Saturday! Choir practice! I love singing. I've finally found something I'm good at. Something I enjoy and won't quit. What else do I love about choir practice? The Tuck Shop! I'd be so hungry, I'd get greedy. With my £1 I could buy two, no, four, no, six packets of crisps, a chocolate bar and a drink. I'd hide in the toilet cubicle and silently but greedily eat five of the six packets of crisps and then emerge back into the hall with only one packet of crisps, a chocolate bar and a drink. I looked normal. And I felt better here than anywhere else. I could eat as much junk as I wanted and no one would know. And I loved singing. I made friends. This is what I wanted to do when I grew up. The one thing I could do that made me feel amazing.

One day, stood in front of my bedroom mirror, I lifted my T-shirt and I noticed my tummy did a funny thing. When

Peace by Piece

I pressed it with my finger, my tummy was soft like dough and when I removed my finger, my tummy would spring back! Ha! That was a new feeling! I liked it! It felt nicer than bones. I went from being so thin you could see my skeleton to a little bit chubby. And I didn't mind. It felt comfy. I was eleven and starting secondary school soon. Being the eldest of four children, I was the first. A new, exciting adventure!

Busy halls, rucksacks, noise and suddenly I discovered boys! Girls were wearing make-up and hairspray and rolling up their grey, pleated skirts to above the knee. They looked silly but boys seemed to like them for it. Another good thing about starting secondary school was lunch money! I could choose and buy whatever I wanted. Now, let's see...

Sausages and mash? Yuk!

Beef Stew? Disgusting!

Pasta and chicken in a creamy white sauce? It looked and smelled like vomit. The pasta had been ruined by all the other ingredients...

Oooh! Chips! Chips and beans? No I have that all the time at home. I'll have chips, mushy peas and non-meaty gravy with a bread cob on the side, a can of Coke and an iced bun for after. I was in heaven. I floated to my table of choice with my tray of delights. My scalp tingled as I tasted each bite. I couldn't even hear the girly chatter at the table. Oh my gosh! This was the best food ever! I was so happy. And I wasn't hungry anymore. I was full! I knew exactly what I was going to eat the next day. And the day after that, and the day after that! And I did.

And even better, Mum was too busy to worry about trying to get me to eat healthy food anymore. She worked a lot so dinner would be something quick. I'd have pasta in plain tomato sauce, no bits! Or chips and baked beans. Or jacket potato and baked beans. Or a cheese sandwich, no butter, and crisps. "You'll turn into a chip!" Dad would say. And to brush off the fact that that was indeed all I ate, I would come

Peace by Piece

back cheekily with, "Yes, tall and slim with a golden tan!"
"Hey fatty bum, bum!" Someone sang to me one day from across the street.
'Am I fat?' I thought. 'Is that bad?'
Oh dear. People had begun to notice I'd put weight on. It had never mattered to me before. Why would it? I was a child. I didn't care about what I looked like. I just wanted to sing and create and read and laugh and daydream. But then I thought about how much I wanted to be a singer. And there were no singers who were famous and fat. The more I thought about this, the more comforting carbohydrates I'd eat, and the fatter I'd become. I only liked a handful of different foods. My mum took me to a doctor. I was referred to a dietician. She gave me a list of all the different types of foods I could eat. She told me of foods I'd never heard of. They terrified me! She showed me a picture of the healthy eating plate. How much carbs, protein and dairy I could have and so on. All I kept thinking was, But I don't like it! Why do I have to change? They can't force me!
She labelled me a lazy eater. She said I was fussy because I didn't like messy food. Like sticky oranges that I'd have to peel or hard apples which would get skin stuck between my teeth. But I knew the truth. I was terrified of food. I had a food phobia. I was too scared to try new things. And food I didn't like would make me feel sick to look at it, smell it, touch it or even be near it.
I started college to study Popular Music. I left my school friends behind me and did my own thing. I made new friends. These new friends were like me. Singers and musicians. Nobody called me fat. Boys seemed to find me attractive. I had boobs and curves. I met my first boyfriend. And as soon as I turned 18 I moved out of the family home to rent a room close to college. Feeding myself didn't seem difficult. I knew how to use a microwave and how to boil pasta.
Now that I could truly be myself and do the things I

loved to do and be with likeminded people, I had become confident. Singing made me feel sexy. Food wasn't such a big deal anymore because the focus had been taken off. And the more people that came into my life the more I would learn about food. The foods I'd never tried before. It would start with adding a herb or a spice. Then pretending I liked something at a friend's house, so as not to be rude, and it turned out that I did like it. So I would start to try more and more vegetables. I still don't like broccoli or mushrooms but hey, I can live without them. I could finally eat out and there'd be more than one thing on a menu that I could eat! Each time I tried and liked something new I would call my mum excitedly and she would tell me how proud she was. She knew more than anyone how much I had overcome. Then I started to cook meat. Roast chicken, diced chicken for a curry, the dreaded bolognaise. I tried chicken, but most of the time I would leave it and only eat the vegetables and potatoes or rice.

I was trying new foods, slowly, by myself. No one was staring because they didn't know. It was easier to just say I'm a vegetarian. And no one would argue with me about that. Then people and restaurants would assume that a vegetarian meal would have to be a goat's cheese dish or a mushroom dish or a quorn dish. I didn't like any of those things. Why would I eat quorn? It is a meat substitute. It has the same taste and texture of meat. And I don't like meat! There would always be only one vegetarian option. Unless I wanted just a side order of chips. I started to look for recipes. Beans, lentils and root vegetables I'd never tried. How exciting! I cooked for friends and lovers and it turned out I had a flair for putting things together. People always complimented my food. I was so happy with myself; I went back to college and started a professional chef's diploma. Before I knew it I was hacking away at chicken carcasses and skinning and de-boning fish! Fish!! Last time I checked I couldn't be near it, see it, smell it. And here I was handling it, admiring it then cutting it up! I had to take photos to prove to myself, and my family that I had done it! I was cooking lamb and beef and pork. The teachers knew I was a vegetarian. They wished I would try the food I was cooking in order to be a better chef. But they didn't force me, or argue with me.

If you're reading this and can relate to neophobia (a phobia of the new) with food, I recommend trying things in your own time. When you're ready. Either alone or with new friends. Order/cook something that you don't know if you like, for someone else, and ask to try theirs. Don't let it be an issue. You don't have to explain yourself. The more times you face your fears, the sooner you will overcome it and you will feel invincible. You can do this.

Now I'm studying pastry. I've always preferred savoury to sweet but apparently I'm good at baking so here I am getting another qualification. Bringing baked goodies home to my wonderful and supportive partner. We have a three-year old son and they're the two loves of my life. I no longer dream of being a singer. It's something I still enjoy and singing has brought me love and self-confidence, but my new dream is to start my own business, selling tea and cake and maybe a nice vegetarian stew, with my talented artist partner displaying his work on the walls. I am so lucky in my life. It turns out I wasn't really a very fat teenager. I just thought I was. I was curvy and sexy! I don't have very much money. In fact, I don't have any. But I have love. I have life. I have a wonderful family. I always have. I have a nice comfy waistline and now I can confidently and proudly say, "I am a natural vegetarian. I just don't like to eat meat." But I do like cooking it. You should try my bolognaise! It's made with love.

Peace by Piece

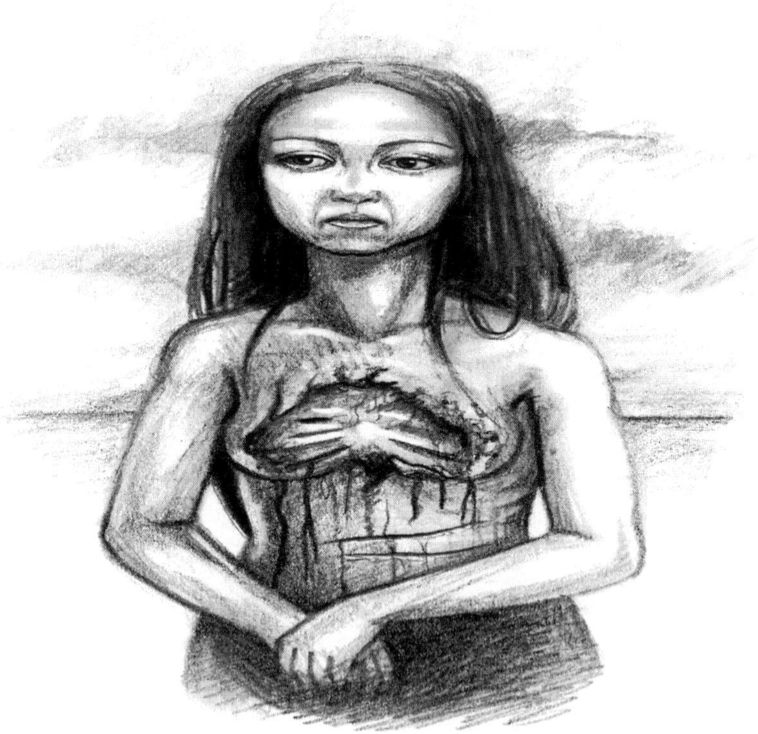

BOOBS, BOSOM, TITS
by Kathleen Pollitt

A square of the softest silk, green fringed with yellow paisley detail.
I had the brainwave in that first 4.30am meditation. After two hours of attempted focus, once back in my room, I found it. Putting the scarf round my back, I crossed it over at the front and tied it behind my neck. My breasts felt pleasingly held. Supported enough so as not to be distracted by smooshy skin-on-skin of boobs on torso, though not quite enough that I wouldn't have to reposition occasionally. I wouldn't have thought to try this makeshift bra in ordinary life, but my schedule was looking quite mellow; Eleven hours of mediation a day, breakfast, lunch, washing, maybe a stroll in the limited wooded area.

I'd woken with the gong at the ridiculous required hour, regarded the simple selection of clothes I'd brought with me, pulled on two jumpers over my pyjamas and put my slippers on for the short, albeit snowy, walk to the hall. My roommate had already left for breakfast. When I had arrived the previous day 'noble silence', as they call it, had already begun so I never did learn her name. Although I was alone, I felt no need to undress in the cold in order to put a bra on to be around a group of people who weren't allowed to look at each other. Once in the hall and attempting to concentrate on the meditation technique, I thought about many things, but mostly about trying not to fall back asleep, and the relationship I'd just started with a man who looks like Tarzan. Terrible timing, how could I not spend the next 10 days obsessing about him? I wore a blanket over my shoulders and absent-mindedly used my hands as a bra while sitting cross legged in rows with 40 or so serene looking women and the same number of men on the other side of the hall. I realised this setting was a rare opportunity to not bother with the confines of a bra. I don't ordinarily give so much thought to my boobs, but in this place of gentle movements and nobody looking at my body following this thought felt like a cosy, simple pleasure.

The scarf ordinarily lived in my violin case, wrapping the violin I never played, it now smelled beautifully wooden around my chest.

Back in the hall the technique was being further explained. Vipassana meditation involves feeling the sensations of your breath on your upper lip as you exhale through the nose. Your mind will wander and you will feel aches and pains but you must try to be equanimous, and observe any uncomfortable or unpleasant sensations with distance. Not reinforcing and worsening the pain by thinking 'ow it hurts', but watching it and allowing it to pass. After three days of focusing one's attention the technique changes and things get more interesting. The technique is explained on nightly video recordings of Goenka, a kind looking old Burmese man. Voice recordings of him chanting soothingly also crackle through the sound system intermittently during meditation sessions. We're advised to slowly sweep our attention over every part of our bodies, feeling the sensations from the crown, down over the face; ears, eye brows, chin, and down across your body, including any slight breeze or itch or contact with fabric, anything. Listening to the body often brings up stored feelings previously ignored. Observing and not rejecting the sensations reflecting your sorrow, your anger and your shame, inadvertently brings greater self-acceptance. With time your awareness of sensations will sharpen. If there are areas you can't feel any sensations at all in, focus your attention, come back to it and consider if this is a troublesome area for you. He refers to these areas as 'blank spots'. If difficult memories are raised, don't force it or become distracted from observing sensations equanimously. Goenka talks about getting into the

Peace by Piece

mind of that body part and feel exactly what it experiences. The idea is that in feeling these stored 'sankharas', as he calls them, you allow them leave you; to stop troubling you. Stored memories are expressed as heat, pain, and itching. The process is like untangling internal knots.

The only kinship is with the ginger cat you aren't allowed to touch, so as not to encourage distracting physical contact. I befriend him, secure in the knowledge that no one will break silence to tell me off. Though we aren't allowed to communicate I get the feeling that people are communicating through the snowmen. By the woods stands a giant snow Buddha someone must have had fun creating while everyone was sleeping, and bit by bit others add to it. By the entrance to the meditation hall, on an expertly made long twig ladder, stands a little climbing snowman that remains unmelted throughout the course. Halfway through the course concentration still proves extremely difficult. This frustrates me as I've come here to try to heal myself for the new relationship I'm starting, before the honeymoon is over and he changes his mind. I don't know quite what I'm fixing, I just feel a dirtiness leftover from past relationships, an uneasiness, that needs cleansing before I can ask someone to love me.

I try having conversations with body parts but am quickly distracted when I don't get the whole-body buzzing sensations that I've heard come with refined practice. Silence is fine, I'm used to silence. Meditation is tough. Silence is comfort; it is disassociation, tuning out. I remembered this when I sat down for the first session. In social situations I have fantasised about being able to be this silent and still.

Though it's not a problem for me to not talk for ten days, occasionally things do slip out, from somewhere inside me directly to my mouth; things my brain doesn't authorise. Perhaps part of a song or something more embarrassing. Men eat and sleep in separate parts of the building to women,

Peace by Piece

their section of the grounds is separated by hedges and fences. Only outside the entrance to the hall do we see men, and there's one I've had the corner of my mind on. I happen to see him nearby one afternoon and, "fuck, he's gorgeous" slips out... quietly, but still. Fantasies about strangers and about Tarzan creep in during these long hours, as do endless thoughts of what I will choose to eat for lunch, replaying of memories, plans for when I get home and many great ideas of things to make and do, but for now I am struggling in a sea of Buddhas.

Days merged and as I get used to the routine my focus begins to refine, and I can lose myself for long stretches of time now.

Towards the end of the course we are informed that 'noble silence' outside of the hall will end, though there are still several meditation sittings to go, so as not to reintroduce us to society too quickly and traumatise us with the lack of stillness. The atmosphere at leaving that session is excitable, and I run away, not ready. Eventually my roommate comes to our room, and I feel comfortable in this one-on-one setting to bond, we talk animatedly and giggle about the experience.

On the subject of how it has gone and why she came she says, "I just wanted to try it, I don't have a lot of specific stuff that I wanted to work on, how about you?"

I'm surprised at her. I start to tell her about my stuff, having assumed most peoples' life stories contain some sort of gruesome drama. I have some silly misplaced smugness about having more negative life experience than this girl, who seems quite sheltered. As if that were a bad thing.

She asked if I had experienced the blank spots Goenka talked about.

"Not so much, except for my boobs, but no one can feel them right?"

She laughed. "Duh, that was the whole practice, observe the blank spots."

Peace by Piece

I wondered why I didn't twig this with so much time to think. Hundreds of hours had passed in that hall. I'd been hearing "expect blind spots and study them", but it didn't even occur to me that this blind spot was a blind spot, so deep was my unawareness. I could feel every part of my body, the smallest sensations, except in my breasts... complete blank. As we speak things start to come up, vivid memories previously locked up. I start to reel with it and am more than grateful for the gong signalling the next meditation. Speaking had started to feel very difficult and abrasive. I wanted my isolation bubble back.

Silent, focused, and listening, I could breathe easy again in the warm safety of the hall with Goenka's mellow, ignorable tones. Comfortably knowing I had several sessions left to hide myself in, I get back in to listening to my body parts, my insides. I begin to realise I am feeling the missing sensations in my breasts, them touching fabric, the slight twinges of pain. It is a curiously novel feeling as though they were a paralysed limb suddenly grown back new nerve endings. I looked deeper, searched harder, observed diligently, making up for lost time and I was gone, remembering.

He tried to take them from me, my core, my womanhood.

He teased and tortured the hopes and dreams of my womb. My womb told me about the physical damage, its heartbreak over lost babies, I saw how this had begun to cause psychosomatic problems in the form of heavy emotions over portrayals of children in danger. I began the healing on this by listening and continued to listen further. There was a time when I told myself my partner calling me 'shit-tits' as an endearment meant we were in a bubble of dare-to-be-mean, hilarious humour that was over the heads of the rest of the world. I offended all of my insides by letting him in. During many an argument he threatened to cut my hair while I slept. Systematically he was taking down all four aspects of

Peace by Piece

my womanhood. Hair, vagina, womb, breasts. As if I wasn't worthy of my most fundamental core, my identity. Before my world, my family, my age, my passions, my truths, before all this, being woman. As though a long line of mothers stretched behind me and he deemed me unworthy to be in it. Not worthy of my innermost purpose, he sought to de-womanise, dehumanise me. I struggle to find the words for how gory the thought of it is. Ripping off the breasts. He tried to take them from me. We fought, he threw me across the room and down the stairs. I came back to the room for my shoes so I could leave the house. He would make me say all sorts of things against myself before maybe giving me what I wanted, somehow he was on top of me again, his knees on my arms so I couldn't move. Not shouting, just calmly mocking like a psychopath full of hate. He spat at me, grabbed my tits and pulled, trying to remove them, bruising me there for a long time.

Back on the outside of my body, I finally realised why the snippets of memory I had of this had always caused such a strong reaction in me, when it hadn't seemed all that different from other things I'd easily locked up, other events seemed more lethal, other words more damaging. For a long time I couldn't go near this one portion of my brain without crying. But now I've looked directly at this place it is getting clearer. I now see being forced to say things against myself as the reason I'm still on the road back to having faith in my own words and voice. I remembered that I'd said something to Tarzan -a real insult to myself that I expected him to laugh at. When I saw that he wasn't going to, I saw that this isn't how normal people interact. This man doesn't hate me and we aren't going to bond over how rubbish I am. Some of the knots have fallen away.

I felt calm for the rest of the meditation. I closed my eyes and saw a painting, an oil painting in the style of Frida Kahlo,

Peace by Piece

a symbolic portrait of a strong looking woman seemingly unaware of her blatant scars; two long knife wounds in the stomach, blood pouring out of the cunt, messily torn flesh where the breasts should have been, ribs exposed. My body remembers physical and psychological hurt. Now, knowing that I will accept its shame and welcome it as a friend, my body has permitted me to see this self-image it has been living with for years.

Observing my sensations and quietly listening gave me an awareness that allowed me to feel in control, not a victim to my issues. It allowed me to identify that the scars were there because of things that happened, not from an inner truth of who I am. Owning that warrior-like image of the exposed rib cage woman explained why my breasts felt like an alien body part and allowed me to start healing my relationship with my body. I left that place feeling a little bit magic, a hell of a lot more connected to my body, and like a woman who loves having tits.

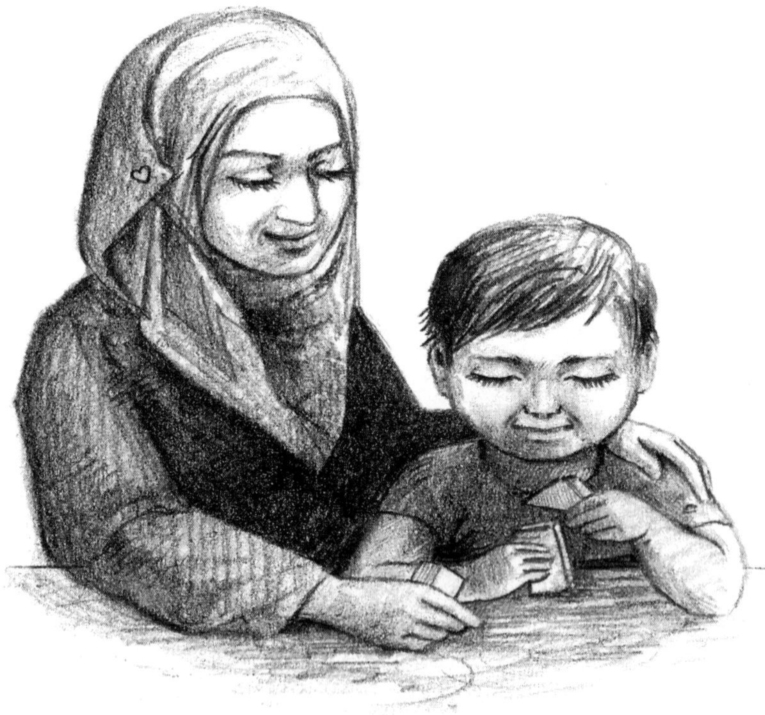

Don't Give Up
by Anonymous

My friend is 30 years old. She is from Tunis. She started out happy because she fell in love. The man she fell in love with is from Pakistan, but he is also English. She came to London as a student, and he came to London for work. That is where they met. They fell in love and he went to Tunis to ask her family for permission to marry her. After they married in Tunis, they moved to Nottingham, where his family also live. She left her family in Tunis.

But when she arrived in Nottingham, his mother was not friendly. His mother didn't like her because she was from Tunis, and she had planned for her son to marry her friend's daughter, not a woman from Tunis. My friend had to learn a new language and new customs, as well as how to be a married woman, and it was very hard for her. Her son was often scared because of the anger in the house. My friend called me, crying, and said she was very sad with her husband. She asked if she could come to me, and said no, you need to stay at home and calm down. I can see you in the café later, but right now you stay with your son because he needs you.

Three days later she was at my home, and she wasn't doing well. Her husband had changed since the marriage, and he was always angry. This effected both she and her son. I told her she could face it, because she is strong and that she can find the change in her life and be happy, that she was lucky to have a good husband. I said sometimes life is like the sea; sometimes it is cool and calm, and sometimes it billows and is strong. I said, "you have quiet volition. I see the changes in you. Your face is ashen and your eyes are swollen from crying. You must to go work—any kind of work, you must not stay at home. Go out with friend or go with your son to the park. You can arrange your life to make it better."

Peace by Piece

But every Sunday she has to the mother-in-law's house so she can see her grandson. But this was hard with the mother in law because she couldn't accept that her son had married a woman other than the one she had chosen for him. One day my friend brought a present for her mother-in-law, but the mother-in-law said it was a present for her daughter, not for her. Then she took all the woman into another room, but made my friend stay behind by herself, because she wasn't welcome there. This continues to happen every Sunday, because she has no choice but to take her son to see his grandparents. But now, instead of it making her cry, she accepts the situation. She is polite, but she doesn't feel like she needs to make it better anymore.

Then, my friend called and told me, "My husband says he is going to work, but he isn't. He goes to another friend's house and watches football. I call him all day, all the time, but he doesn't answer his phone." I told my friend not to call him all the time, because some men don't like to be bothered like that. I explained that maybe sometimes he is busy and can't talk to you. She says he is still always angry at home and he doesn't help at all with their son. She has to do everything: take care of the shopping, the child, even GP appointments. I told her I think her husband works too much and is too busy, and that's what makes him so angry. He isn't angry at her, he is stressed and frustrated.

My friend listened to me, and started working at the school her son goes to. This has made her feel much better, and her son is better too, because he's in school. She is there every day from one o'clock to two-thirty, and it's been very good for her not to be home alone all the time.

Her husband does love her, and she's mostly happy in the marriage now. She doesn't like how busy he is, or that he has to work in other countries sometimes. He works so hard to give them a nice life, but sometimes she is too lonely or sad to understand that. She will stay with her husband because their son needs a mother and a father, both. Although sometimes the son gets upset because the father is angry. When their son comes over to play with my son, I ask him if he loves both his mom and his dad, and he says both, but, "mom, and mom, and mom!" Sometimes, the father takes the son swimming, and that is good for both of them.

It is important to get out of the house, and not stay at home alone all the time. I miss my family too, but if I get out of the house, I don't focus on problems or things that make me sad. I go to a café, or I go out with friends. All marriages have problems, all kinds of problems. But you can work through them by finding other outlets to make you feel better. You don't have to give up on your marriage, just find a way to make your life better.

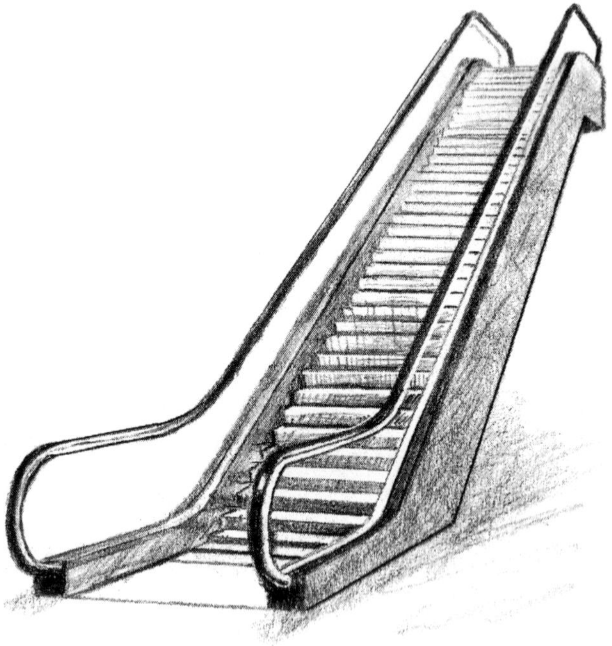

ONE WAY TICKET
by Mina Fatemi

It's four o'clock in the morning, when the cold October night still has its paws on the benighted city.
It's four o'clock, just before the dawn, and as I stand in the queue with a one-way ticket in my hand, I feel the bitter taste of death in my mouth as I think of all those who are lined up to be hanged at four o'clock, on another cruel morning in the future, because they decided never to stand where I am standing, holding a one-way ticket.

I'm in the airport, surrounded by whoever still matters to me, in the land that once was my home.

There is no scent in the air; not from the branded perfumes people usually wear when they go to the airports to set off, or see off, nor the scent of hundreds of bunches of flowers handed in, or out, to travellers.

There is no sound to memorise. The world stands still, with only me moving toward a vague destiny and yet, the next moment it is me, still, motionless amongst a crowd of passers-by, rushing toward their existence. How alienated I feel, how inappropriate my presence. Is this my home town?

In the midst of these strange feelings there are images here and there of faces I recognize, people I love so much, hearts I am hurting so much. My family, who are going to be a memory from now on, will always be my family even if we never again sit around a table together or breathe in the same air.

There is an escalator waiting for my tentative steps to take me to the world I belong to more. An escalator which is the bridge between two worlds, the border between captivity and freedom.

Surrounded by all my beloved members of family, I can sense a presence behind the walls, someone tearfully wishing he could hug me for the last time, ending five years of love

Peace by Piece

and alas, wishing he could come out of the secret box for once and forever.

There are many things to be left behind, but I cannot focus and count. The moment my mother hugs me and I see only two red eyes are left in her thin face, and she whispers in my ear:

"Take care daughter. Come back soon. Don't ruin your life".

My dad starts crying so hard, crying harder than I've ever seen him cry in my 28 years with him.

"How can you leave us and go like this? 6 months is too long. Don't waste yourself in stranger lands."

I feel a slash in my heart. It's my biggest lie: 6 months. 6 months in which he stayed in bed, melting of sorrow, feverish with the fear of never seeing me again.

They are quietly begging me to stay. In their hearts they are shouting: don't, don't, don't and I am numb. Can't hear, can't sense, can't talk and… can't stay.

I break into pieces of fear and guilt.

Where am I going?

What am I doing?

My sister, with a face as innocent as that little girl who used to run with me down our streets of childhood, stands there embracing her little son with a look as serene as ever, but her words pierce through my hesitant lies and breaks the silence.

"You are not coming back soon, are you?"

Where on this earth can I have a sister with whom I share all my childhood memories? She knows which day of childhood I am talking about by every emotion on my face and we laugh our heads off as we remember every childish romance we had with neighbourhood boys.

Where on this earth can I find a woman who cares for me as my mom does, and a man I can trust as much as my dad? Will I ever see my parents again, before wrinkles cover all the familiar lines of their faces, and aging ailments wash away all our common memories, one after another, from their minds?

I know I am going to miss a lot of what makes life worth living. I am not going to be there when my nephew walks for the first time, stumbling over any invisible bit, when he talks and learns to say my name. I will be a face in a photo framed on the windowsill and a voice from far, far away. I know I've lost the chance to spin him around while holding his tiny hands in mine. This is the last time he will give me that familiar look with his round brown eyes. Next time he sees me, he will only see a stranger.

When will I stealthily listen to my brother's much-loved music tapes and sneakily read my sister's books, the way I used to do before I reached the age I was actually allowed to do so.

Is this last time I will see them? There is a bitter answer I don't want to think of.

That is me, walking up the stairs, getting on that bridge. I watch myself as if from a distance. I take my first uncertain steps on a fragile road, carrying the heavy burden of my heritage with me. My mission is to be an ambassador, always, wherever I go and whoever I become. I taste my mother's thoughts on my tongue, thoughts she never dared to convert to words. She who is standing down there, getting smaller and smaller as I go away, and when I can see only two light reflections of tears behind her glasses, my own tears of guilt pour out.

I know I am nothing similar to daughter she wanted. I am a rebel, a stranger, a foreigner. I am going to be a foreigner forever. To my own people, and for all those who I am going to meet from now on. I get on the bridge and look back to wave for the last time. Behind the thick glass of the airport walls, there are eyes crying for me. At four o'clock on an October morning, I am leaving hearts beating so heavily, so sadly, for one who chose to go forever.

There are light reflections everywhere I almost can't see anymore. I start to see tears everywhere. On the stairs, on the floors, and on faces I blindly pass by.

I evaporate in front of their eyes in the crowd. I turn into a ghost whose presence is not to be sensed except in surreal life. I start to die in everybody's mind, even mine. There is a snapshot of me on the lingering escalator, carved into their minds, wearing my black and white hijab for the last time. It's the last time...

I feel the sky on my head for the last time.

I am nervous about getting caught for not having a proper hijab on, for the last time.

"For the last time..." starts to contain a tingling of joy.

I start to shed in the twilight of the border. I am a survivor of revolution and war. I am the survivor of misogyny and discrimination. I am the survivor of infidelity, someone who deserved to die for what she could not believe in any more.

The black moving belt, like a rope of rescue, carries me toward the liberty I am thirsty for.

Taboos have chained me to the escalator and there is no going back.

I drop the nationalism and Arianism in me and racism lets me go.

Liberty multiplies in my cells.

I bury all the unfinished, dead dreams and wishes under the rubber stairs.

There was once a woman living in me whose passion was to die for her country. But she never dared to show her face in any movement or campaign as the threat was so much to bear. There was a girl in me who knew she was going to be the first Iranian female president, but she never had the chance to get near what she longed for. There was a little child whose dream was to be God, for those whom have not been created yet and for those universes which have not experienced existence yet.

Peace by Piece

I know now that being born in the territory of one country does not create brotherhood and sisterhood, and having grown up under one flag does not bring up descendants with the same attitudes. We as humans, who are thrown up by nature somewhere in the world, deserve to find our own compatriots defined by us, and only us.

Like a bird following signs in the sky, I let my instincts guide me to my fate.

I go, and I know I am running away, but not from a piece of land in which I felt the nostalgia of all those who look back at a country they no longer belong to. I run, but not from a lost nation whose outlook strangled me nearly to death. I run from myself and all those who lived in me once. I run so I can forgive that child for not becoming a God, that girl for never getting anywhere close to her dream of presidency, and that woman for not getting shot in the green movement. I run to find out where on the earth I can sense the truth of humanity and share it with all likeminded souls.

I bury the old me at the border, and a stranger steps into the land where she believes it is possible to breathe, where she can be the little Goddess of her own life.

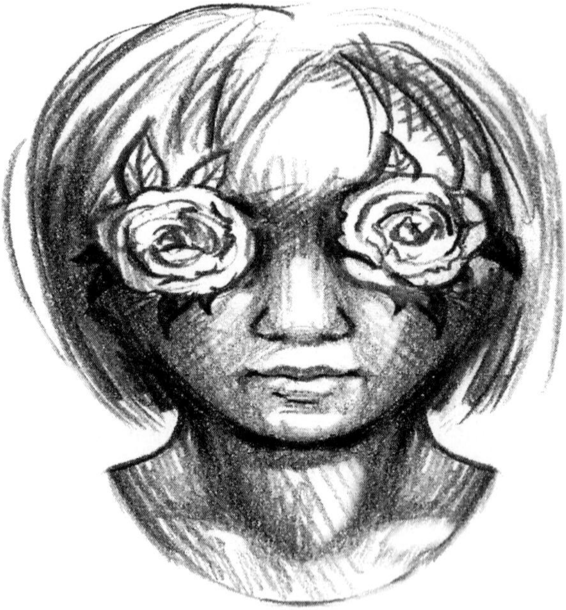

THE GIRL IN THE ROSE GARDEN
by Clare Barton

June 1978, Nottingham, England.

I woke up this morning feeling hot as the light streamed in through my golden curtains. They have a repeating pattern of large gold circles, which had been sewn onto them. Each circle resembled the sun.

My mum was already in my bedroom. She clomped on my wooden floorboards as she headed towards my wardrobe and threw open the door.

"I think it will be best if you go to your Granddad's today. I'm busy and I have things to do at home," she said.

It already felt stifling inside my bedroom. I knew the day was going to be as hot as it was yesterday. To my dismay, my mum pulled out my best summer dress from the wardrobe. She held it up, presenting it to me as if it were a gift.

"It doesn't fit me anymore and I don't want to go to Granddads," I said.

"It's still brand new, you've hardly worn it. I need to get my money's worth... now hurry up!" she said.

Reluctantly I started to get dressed, and she forced the outgrown dress over my head. I managed to get my arms through the sleeveless holes, which dug into my under arms.

The day felt wrong, the dress felt wrong and the weather was too hot.

But, in spite of all this, I also thought that if I did go to my Granddad's house today, I could go outside into his rose garden. Will she be there too? Sometimes she would meet me there.

When asked, my family promised me that I would get to see her someday, the girl who sometimes came to play with me. They also told me that they didn't know when this would be. That's what they always told me.

Peace by Piece

But I saw her without them knowing and when I did, I knew who she was. But if the grown-ups were there too, I pretended I didn't see her, and she seemed to know that meant I couldn't come out to play. .

I thought perhaps my Granddad knew and he had arranged for me to spend the day with her at his house. Maybe that was why I was going there today. The thought of this cheered me up, and it made the sweltering car journey to my Granddads house more bearable.

"Perhaps you can ask your Granddad if you can watch 'Rainbow' on his TV today?"

When I arrived at my Granddads house, my mum was in a hurry, so she left me in the rose garden and waved goodbye from the small wooden gate.

Four years old, and here I was, all alone in the rose garden. Being an only child, spending time on my own was a common occurrence. So, I had learnt to play quietly and to amuse myself. I decided to wait here for a while, to see if she came today. I wondered if she knew I was here?

The heat from the midday sun started to feel unbearable. The longer I stood there waiting, the more I began to feel exposed. With my dress too short, it felt as though my legs and thighs were being repeatedly slapped, so hard that a scalding mark was being imprinted upon them. So I decided I couldn't wait any longer and went inside to find some shade, to escape from the condescending sun.

The green, wooden front door to my Granddad's corner council house was left open expectantly today.

Once I was inside I knew that he had slung his door wide open in the chance of catching any breeze drifting in to cool the house. But there was no chance of that. It was just as hot inside as it was out.

"I can't stand this weather! It's too hot to play outside."

"Well, I can't change the weather," he said

"Is she coming to the rose garden today?" I said.

"No, no one is coming today. No one ever does."
"Can I watch Rainbow on TV?" I said.
"No, you can't watch Rainbow today. I want to watch England play the West Indies at Cricket. I don't want to miss any part of the final, just because you want to watch those stupid puppets!"

I flung myself down onto an armchair, and sighed with boredom. I didn't have many toys at Granddad's house. So, I played games that relied solely on my imagination. I began to feel frustrated, irritable and tired, lacking in inspiration.

Then, in what seemed like the next moment, I realised that time had passed me by, as the television set was blaring away with the afternoon Cricket match, which had my Granddad fully absorbed.

I noticed that the light shining in through the net curtains is no longer glaring. The wooden table is dappled with sunlight from the above window. The soft shadows flicker in the corner of the room, as the curtains move in the gentle wind. The room feels cooler and the heat is less intense. I know that the sun is no longer scalding. So I decide to take the chance and step back outside into the rose garden.

The rose garden consists of square concrete slabs and the odd few steps which allow access around the garden, so that the roses can be attended to, or just simply admired.

The colours from the roses meet my eyes in an abundance of pastel softness. The floral aroma drifts lightly from the pinks, corals, yellows and reds. Most of the roses are in full bloom and at their best.

My Granddad has told me that he doesn't mind if I pick the roses that are nearly finished, nearly dead. But I should leave the blossoming roses to flourish.

I notice that some of the petals on the older Roses are becoming withered and darkened around the edges, and a few have shriveled up, turned brown and fallen off the stem onto the square slabs. I pull a few petals off one of the

Peace by Piece

drooping roses and watch as the rest of the rose falls easily apart onto the concrete.

I don't think she will come to the rose garden today. I thought maybe it was because I wasn't wearing the right dress. But now I don't think my Granddad really knows who she is.

I glanced behind me toward the house and I try to see in through the front room window. I can still hear the Cricket match on the television. The spectators all start to applaud at once, which escalates, as if they are all clapping with wooden hands. I am sure my Granddad is still fully absorbed.

Being careful of the thorns, I find myself amid the tender ripe roses. Their pastel hues seemed to radiate a delicate aroma and I notice that near to the heart of the flowers, the petals are folded so neatly, that I wondered what possibly could be hidden away through their pleats?

Is there something they're not telling me? Is it something I need to know?

I choose a rose and I slowly pull at one of the fresh petals, which needed a firmer tug before it would leave the flower. The rest of the rose remains intact. So I pull harder, which removes another petal. As I fondle the departed petals between my fingers and thumb, I notice that their succulent texture feels moist and spongy. I then catch the scent of the flower which smells greater as the rest of the petals abandon the stem.

My thoughts drift into a daydream as I quietly maintain the habit of plucking at the flowers, until I feel the dispersion of each one. My notions gradually become more lucid as I lose myself in my daydreams.

She came skipping down my Granddads path, which is an aisle to White-as-Snow summer flowers that match her sandals with a Cuban bell that clicked and clopped as she danced. The dress she wore was white cotton that billowed as she swayed. Around her neck she wore a bronze crucifix

Peace by Piece

with a figure of Christ. In her hair she wore pretty hair slides, equal on either side of her head. Her hair and smile glowed in the sunshine.

We held each other's hands and spun around together, laughing as we swirled. We hopped around the rose garden, leaping from slab to slab. Suddenly, she would stop to gasp in admiration and would cup her hands and hold her chosen flower closely. She'd breath in slowly and smile as she inhaled the floral scent.

Suddenly she stepped back and turned decisively to face me.

"My name is Agnes Theresa Sullivan," she said.

"No. You can't be," I said. "She's dead!"

"Yes, I know," she said

Agnes was my Great Grandma's name. A family member had shown me photograph of her, but I had never met her, of course. She had died well before I was born.

"But, I do know who your mother really is," she said, whilst holding her small, bronze, crucifix between her fingers, close to her chest.

We stared at each other intensely for a short time, as I accepted her solidity. I was almost certain she was telling the truth, as she was holding her cross so close to her chest.

"I have got to go now," she said. And then she was gone.

I became conscious that I had finished off most of the roses, even the ones yet to really bloom. I stared down at the square slabs on the ground.

The contrast, from the flat, dull, grey, hard concrete, against the colorful sprinkling of the pastel petals looked so beautiful that I instantly became overjoyed and pleased with my creation. I bent down and quickly scooped up a handful of petals and threw them all over myself in delight. I pretended it was confetti being thrown by guests at my wedding.

I stepped backwards, allowing myself room to view the larger picture.

Peace by Piece

The sky suddenly darkened as a dull, blue light was cast upon the garden. I gasped in shock at my surroundings.

The rose garden was in a state of devastation.

There was a foreboding atmosphere which hung around the garden in stagnant clouds, filled with a humid hostility.

The roses were now sketches of a stark mesh. Their shameful stature provided no pleasure, for they have lost their appeal. The deserted petals are scraps of ripped ribbons, which have become ravaged into piles of bruised despair.

I feel breathless as I devour the regret of the ruined flowers.

I know now that she will never come to the rose garden again.

My main worry now was not to let my Granddad see his ruined roses. I really wished I could have watched Rainbow on TV, so the roses wouldn't have been spoiled today.

I thought of trying to blame my cousin, but she wasn't here. I briefly thought that sellotape might solve my problem, but I knew there wouldn't be enough.

Then I heard a motor rev as a car pulled up outside the gate. I jumped off the slabs onto the garden path, so I wasn't found among the petal-ruins. I hoped it wasn't my mum in the car. But, I instantly knew it was, when I saw the curves of the Navy Blue Morris Miner.

"Come on, I'm in a hurry to get back. Your cousins have come to visit, they're waiting for you at home," she said.

Quickly I climbed into the car, because I didn't want to give her any reason to get out. She glanced at the rose garden as we were pulling off, but, thankfully the hedge shielded the destroyed blooms from her sight.

I was relieved to be inside the car, on the light, blue, warm leather seats, which burned and stuck to my bare legs.

I never saw the girl again, that used to meet me in the rose garden.

My Granddad never mentioned his ruined roses, and it

was almost as if it didn't happen.

A few years later, my Granddad gave me a crucifix. He told me it had belonged my Great Grandma, Agnes. I thought it looked like the same one that the girl was wearing around her neck, in the rose garden. I've kept it, but I've never worn it.

I realised, since that day in the Rose garden, that I couldn't change the past, what is done, is done. Once something beautiful is ruined and destroyed, it may not be possible to atone for the damage. Family can sometimes pass on burdens to their children and occurrences can often go unexplained. Secrets are often kept hidden.

But, this does not mean you have to accept them. You can have your own truth, your own memories, your own rose garden.

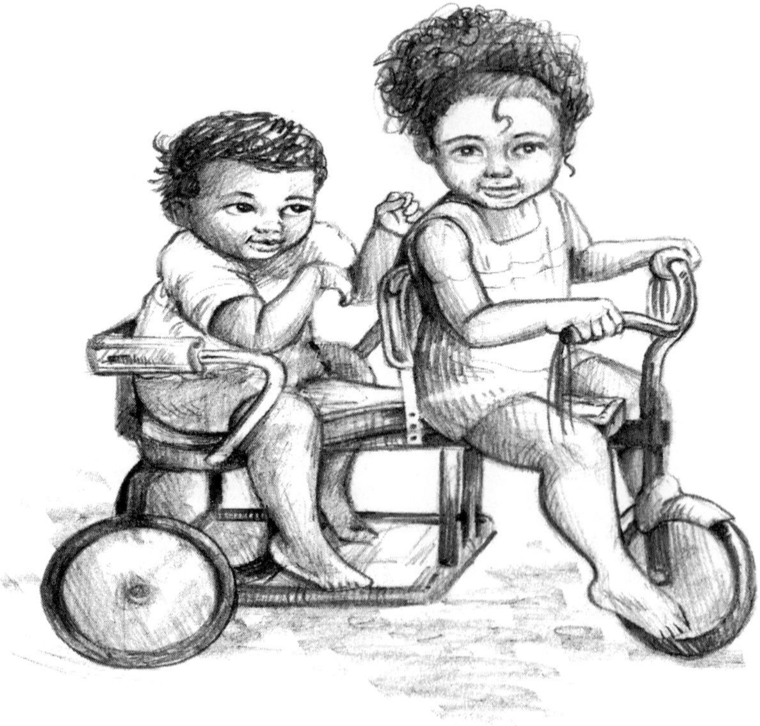

SUNDAY DINNER
by Rastarella

We played silently upstairs in our bedroom, in the dark with only the natural light from the window to help us see. We sat opposite each other tapping the balloon back and forth. It wasn't allowed to touch the floor and we weren't allowed to move; it was our special game. We tried to stifle our giggles as we watched each other stretch out our bodies to tap the balloon. We weren't allowed to make any noise or bangs, because last week we were taught another lesson when mother said our laughter had woken her up. The wooden spoon had eventually snapped apart across my back, which had vexed her more. My sister was dutifully sent to get the belt. Then it was double beats, one for making noise, another for breaking the spoon. The belt buckle was still imprinted on my upper arm. I ran my finger over it as I became lost in thought. The balloon fell to the floor. Game over.

We were called down for Sunday dinner, and we scrabbled to get to our feet as quick as we could. If she had to call our names twice we knew what would happen.

2 hours later...

"Eat your bloody dinner!" My step father shouted. "You two are so ungrateful, think about all those starving children in Africa." His face got redder by the second. I focused on the sprouts of hair that covered the top of his predominantly large English nose, (I needed to find some kind of humour in the midst of torture), hair was meant to be grown in your nose, not on top. His words kept repeating like a broken record, but we had to pretend that this was the first time we were hearing his commands, his whiskey and cigarette toxic breath imposing on my ear drums, seeping into my soul. If the truth be known I would rather be starving in 'Africa' than have to eat all this disgusting stodge and slop again and again, week in, week out.

But something about this time seemed different. Usually we would just ignore the demands of my stepfather, then my mother would come in and attack us with any object she could find, taking out her rage on our young and defenceless bodies. She would even give us a ten second head start after we had emptied our cold and congealed dinners into the bin. One time my poor sister somehow found herself stuck in the shoe cupboard, and ended up being target practice for my mother's throwing skills, shoe heels being expertly flung towards my sister's face and body, while I was made to stand and watch.

But this evening was unusual, yes he shouted, but this time we were told we had to sit there and eat everything, everything. He turned off the lights and left us in the dining room. In the dark. The sun had been replaced with a sky filled with dark clouds. We sat opposite each other, elbows off the table, no water, no talking and no microwave. Hours seem to go by and the room began to get cold. I looked across at my sister's face and she stared back at me. We knew we weren't allowed to talk, they would hear us, and we would get punished. My eyes drew down to her bowl. She had somehow managed to finish her dinner and now had to eat the thing she hated most in the world, Trifle. I was trailing behind because I was still battling the last remains of my dinner, the dreaded tag team of Leek and Marrow, home grown and overcooked. My throat simply refused to accept these alien vegetables, my stomach waving the white flag in advance. Usually I was allowed to throw them away and then I was denied pudding. No, not this evening, I had to eat everything if I knew what was good for me.

The only way I could contact my sister was by discreetly kicking out my leg to touch hers. 'Eat,' I willed her on with

Peace by Piece

my eyes, 'it will be over once we just eat,' I told her, trying to remind myself at the same time. I knew how much she hated trifle, every time she knew that was the reward for finishing her dinner she would leave as much as she could so that she didn't have to eat it. They had tricked us today, saying it was to be rice pudding and jam, warm and comforting, which happened to be one of our favourites since arriving into this cold and depressing country.

He stormed back in just as my sister was pushing the trifle around her bowl, it wasn't fooling anyone, not even her. It wasn't going anywhere except in her mouth. He stood over us and said that we had been at the dinner table for far too long, that we had five minutes left to eat before our mother entered the room. That familiar sense of impending dread took over. My sister looked at me and I looked at her. We could do this, we had to do this. Hold your nose and swallow, just don't think about it.

My mouth started to water as the fork came up to my lips, holding a flaccid piece of cold leek. I put it inside and tried to swallow, but my jaw clamped down and refused to play ball. My throat locked, and my mind pleaded with my body to stop resisting. I started to feel hot and dizzy. I looked over to my sister who by then had tears rolling down her face as she took in spoonful's of trifle, trying to eat it as fast as she could. Then her expression changed into one I had seen many times before: fear.

She vomited, then I vomited. You know what happens when you see someone else puking up, the smell alone is enough to trigger off more of the same. Well, that's exactly what happened. We both started to puke, up came the remains of our Sunday dinners.

Our stepfather stood there and watched, then shouted to our mother in the living room that we had been sick.

Her reply came back cold, calculated and blunt. "Make them eat it".

Peace by Piece

Even he looked slightly alarmed at her response. We stared at each other, begging our minds to be blank because we both knew that God could read our thoughts and any bad ones about our parents would be punished. He went into the living room, spoke to our mother briefly, then walked back to our table of doom. I looked across at my sister and she had food around her mouth and on her top, and vomited lumps of trifle lay on top of the bowl. I dared to look down at my plate, and saw food I had eaten a few hours before now lay splattered across the tablecloth. It wasn't a pretty sight for either of us.

I'll never forget his words, said in manner of complete normality. "You scrape your trifle on top of her plate and take the food into the kitchen." For a brief second I thought that because we had showed true grit and determination in trying to eat the veg from hell and the sloppy trifle, we were being given a reprieve. But he continued. "You will eat it. In the morning for breakfast, I'll make you some lovely home-made fritters before you go to school." He then whistled and walked back into the living room, leaving my sister and I to wash and dry the dishes.

I woke up and heard the birds singing. It was Monday again, time for school. I loved school, it gave me a chance to be like the other children. I could run, play, laugh and study, all without feeling the fear that surrounded my heart as soon as the school bell rang for the last time at the end of each day. I made my bed, then went to wash my face in the bathroom. Another night of broken sleep had left me looking tired. He had come to get me again as he often did, using the adjoining bathroom to pee then prodding me until I was awake. I had entered their bedroom, tiptoeing in as instructed.

As I lay there I took myself into my own special enchanted land where I was free as a bird, my wings taking me anywhere I wanted to go, surrounded by peace & beautiful creatures. As my innocence continued to be stolen from me in the real world on a daily basis, in my special place there was no one to hurt me. Only goodness and beings who loved me. As his rough and callused hands violated my body, my mother slept in the same bed with her back turned, seemingly oblivious to my plight. I had no one to help me, but at least I had my special place. The part of me nobody could touch. After he had finished, he hugged me hard and whispered that he loved me. I tiptoed back into my bedroom, feeling discarded like yesterday's newspaper.

I realized I was still standing in front of the mirror, and I had my hair in my hands. Lost in thought, I had pulled it out again. I quickly unclenched my hands and wrapped the strands with toilet paper and flushed it down the toilet. I had to get ready for school, and it would soon be time for breakfast.

He was in a good mood. I could smell the oil frying as I came down the stairs, and my sister was already at the dining table. We looked at each other and I saw my sadness and determination reflected back at me. We had spoken before we had fallen asleep, and had decided we would pretend that we were at the best party in the world, and that the breakfast served would be a special delicacy from a far-away magical land. We had trained our minds to cope with so much already over the years, this breakfast would be a breeze.

He put our oily vomit fritters on the plate, and we looked at the time. We had ten minutes to eat them before we had to walk to primary school. We looked at each other and started to eat, and this time it was so easy! Our delicacies fantasy had tricked our mouths, throats and minds into submission. We were done in less than 5 minutes. Relief.

As we thanked him and kissed him bye, we left the house knowing we had overcome another one of our trials. We held hands as we crossed the road, then half walked, half jogged to school. We could be like the other kids for a few hours. We had school dinners to look forward to, as well. That was always a treat. I could never understand why so many other children complained about them.

My childhood and teenage years could only be described in one word: Carnage. Being manipulated and abused in a foreign country with no one to help you or even notice your pain was a very hard pill to swallow. It led to many mental health issues for numerous years as I dug deep to overcome the dark shadows of my past. Having no one to rely on from such a young age changes your views, not only of yourself, but of those around you. It took courage to speak up and confront the memories that tormented me for years, but I was determined to break free and find my true self. The little girl who had to endure such horror deserved to be protected. But she was failed. In finding peace I was able to soothe her. In finding self-love, I was able to heal her, and in speaking about my experiences I was able to give her a voice. She mattered, and it was never my fault.

Time never stands still but it is a great healer. The day I decided to take those first few steps towards healing so that I could stop hurting was the hardest, but also the best thing I could have ever done for myself. Even though some days I wished I could fall into an eternal sleep, deep down I knew I wanted to live. I had to keep on going, and eventually, in those moments of deep darkness I stopped looking for the light and slowly became the light. In seeking professional help I stopped blaming myself and gained self-worth. I was reborn.

For anyone out there reading this I would like you to know that you too deserve to live your best life, you too can break free from the bonds that hold you down. You too can learn to laugh, trust and be loved the right way. Happiness is your birth-right. Self-love is One love and One love is self-love.

Still We Rise.

Peace by Piece

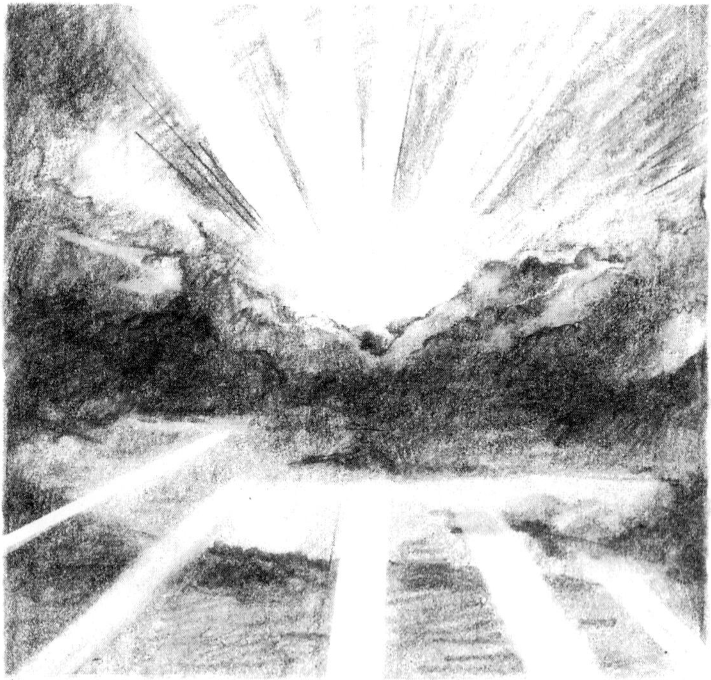

SILENCE IS LOUD
By Sarah

"I hate you!" I say, the anger that seems to forever lurk in my veins bursting forth.

"I hate you too," my father replies in a calm voice as he heads downstairs, leaving me standing in the hall, frozen to the spot. I am thirteen years old and have known for a while that my father is a mean and spiteful man, but I'm still shocked at his response to my outburst. Parents aren't supposed to tell their kids they hate them back.

I walk into the bedroom I share with my older sister and sit on my bed, gazing unseeingly out of the window. I sit alone, feeling that familiar and harrowing stab of pain and loss. Loss for what I know I will never have, but haven't yet accepted. I have been raised with harsh and cruel words. I have been undermined, criticised and told terrible things about who I am my whole life. I have no self-esteem or self-worth and I don't think I really even like myself. Because if my own parents don't like me, then why would I?

My father reminds my sisters and I on a daily basis that we are 'good for nothing', 'useless', 'stupid' and a slew of other delightful things. Mum is not safe from his cruel words either, but this doesn't stop her from constantly comparing us to the perfect dutiful daughters of her friend, or complaining to our relatives about how inadequate we are. Side by side, my father and mother shower us with verbal and emotional abuse. I can barely articulate how much this hurts nor try to measure the damage inflicted.

School is no better. I have a few friends but one of them has recently taken to whispering to the others and looking at me pointedly when doing so. I can't imagine she's saying anything nice. My stomach twists in misery whenever I see her but I don't know how to make her stop so I pretend not to notice. I'm not sure how long this will work.

Peace by Piece

I stay quiet, which is a whole other problem. Some think I'm shy, some think I'm aloof. I'm scared and I'm anxious. I have learnt that silence is my best defence but it is also my own prison because when you are quiet for too long, speaking becomes harder and harder. So I am stuck in a vicious cycle as I keep my thoughts and feelings hidden away. However, I am lucky enough to have discovered an outlet.

I write poems. I try to make sense of my sad and pathetic life, of the anger and hurt engraved in the heart of me, through words. And I listen to music. I go into the front room, away from my parents, and I sit in the dark with headphones on. I escape for a couple of hours. From my life and from myself.

Sitting on my bed now, I glance at the stack of books on the desk about The Beatles. When my eldest sister was home for the summer from university, she bought back with her their CDs and we spent evenings in her room listening to them. I've become obsessed with all things Beatles and want to know everything about them. George is my favourite. The quiet Beatle. I grab a book and am away.

It's 7:25 and my sister, Nikki and I are in our room. She puts her coursework to one side and I watch as she leaves the room quietly to head downstairs. After a few minutes, I too head for the stairs. I move slowly. On the bottom step, I crouch and move off the step into a shuffle. The living room door has a pane of glass set into it and I am careful not to be seen. Once past the door, I creep to the front room where Nikki has already turned the TV on. The TV is old, the images are all in black and white and the dials click loudly when turned. We grin at each other in the ghostly glow of the screen and I take a seat on the sofa. Top of the Pops is about to start. Nikki turns the volume to low and sits down, both of us leaning eagerly towards the TV to see who the first act will be. I'm hoping for Robbie Williams, she'd prefer Boyzone. It's Cleopatra...

Peace by Piece

Towards the end of the show, we hear the living room door open and Nikki leaps at the TV, turning it off and plunging the room into total darkness. She slides back onto the sofa and we hold our breath. Our father walks into the room and switches the light on. Nikki and I blink against the harsh glare but stay quiet, not making eye contact with him. My father doesn't ask us why we are sitting in the dark. Instead, he walks slowly to the window where he draws the curtain to one side and peers out at the street. He stays like this for a few minutes. Nikki and I roll our eyes at each other. Finally he turns and exits the room, leaving the light on. We hear him go back into the living room and finally the TV is back on but the credits are rolling and we've missed the number one act! We sigh and head upstairs together. Nikki slips the headphones to her personal stereo on and resumes her coursework. The sounds of Boyzone blare out and I shake my head to myself. I pull up a chair to the hi-fi that Nikki, myself and Barge bought a couple of years ago much to the hypocritical disapproval of our parents. I stick my headphones into the jack and press play on the CD that's already in there. I lean back and close my eyes.

I may not have the types of self-belief that make for a well-rounded person, I may struggle with my anxiety and insecurities for years to come, but I have my love for music and words, I have two sisters to soften the harshness of my life and I have spirit. One day it will be free.

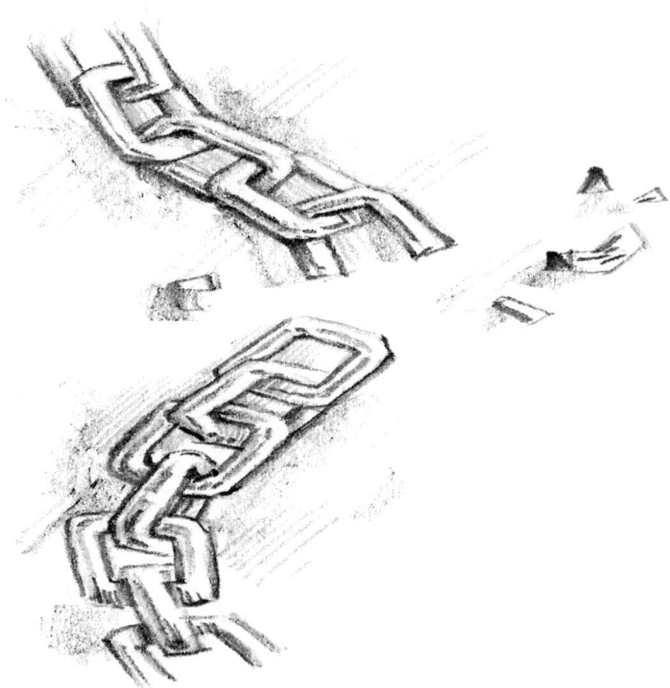

Peace by Piece

Reflections
by TJ

The late afternoon sun streamed in through the patio windows, bathing the threadbare carpet in golden light. Lazing around in the illuminated patches were two cats, warm puddles of fur spilling out in the oppressive August heat, too exhausted from the heat to fight with each other. I lounged out on the sofa in light, cotton pyjamas, auburn hair tied back messily off my neck. The long expanse of summer following my thirtieth birthday seemed to pass too slowly, a swamp of worries and concerns over my future rather than the carefree relaxation it should have been.

The moment I picked up my laptop from the floor hadn't been anything special – I was simply trying to while away the boredom – but it's funny how a moment can change everything, can change that warm, summer glow into piercing spotlights that throw you centre-stage.

I casually flicked between tabs to my emails, not expecting anything new. It was a routine, a silly habit I had developed, though news from work had stopped weeks ago when I had been signed off with a rare form of migraine that left me paralysed on one side. Yet another reason my future was in doubt. But my heart skipped a beat as I saw it.

I set my computer back on the table and began to pace, my bare feet treading their usual pattern across the room. Not that it would make any difference – the decision had already been made.

Since my very first French lesson as a seven year old, I've dreamt of teaching. Even in my darkest moments, it was a goal that kept pushing me on.

And so I paced around the living room, knowing that this single moment could destroy everything, destroy me. A single moment that had the power to change my life forever.

My heart thumped in my chest, convinced the email

would vindicate my former teachers and colleagues; I would never pass, never be good enough, never have the temperament or work ethic... years upon years of baggage that unpicked every compliment, every small achievement. It seemed certain that my dreams of teaching were never meant to be. At every key point, all my plans had unravelled, leaving me seven years later, still a newly qualified teacher without having finished my induction.

There had been a time when anything was possible; a respectable university despite disappointing grades, a perfect teaching placement on my year abroad... that girl would never have doubted her ability to do anything.

I tried to channel that sense of hope and invulnerability as I made a cup of tea. Things had changed over the past few months, I had changed. Surely I had proven myself? I had a job at a school where I was valued and colleagues who genuinely cared about me. I had a head-teacher who knew about all that baggage and who was prepared to accept it. I had lesson observations, quality-assured paper evidence that graded me as a "good" teacher (or at least that I could teach good lessons – not always the same thing). It was there in black and white.

I made my way back to the computer, my hands curled around the scalding cup of tea. Somehow, it seemed ludicrous to be drinking something hot whilst sweltering like this, but there was something reassuring about it. I sat back down, trying to keep my trembling arms from betraying me and spilling tea everywhere. Slowly, I set it on the table and lifted the computer back to my knee. How much longer could I put it off?

It was a simple click on an email. I'd dealt with worse – far worse.

In the back of my mind, I wondered if it was those ghosts I was really afraid of, still rattling their chains around my throat, threatening to silence me once more. I could hear them whispering old lies in my ears, eating away at what little self-confidence I had left.

"You can't teach if you don't have children of your own... The education system doesn't need damaged women like you, you're an embarrassment... You shouldn't be allowed to work with children." The voices taunted and jeered at me, even now.

I gritted my teeth and looked back to the screen in grim determination. I hadn't let him win then, and I wouldn't let him win now. Counselling, working with men, teaching children the same age as the little girl I had lost…. I could deal with a silly computer screen.

Hesitantly, I clicked on the email, or at least thought I did – my panicked, sweaty fingers resulted in three attempts – and allowed my eyes to skim over the screen.

Once, twice… I read the words time and time again, hardly daring to believe them, waiting for the punchline. Shaking, I followed the link, frantically entering the username and password.

A moment passed, a moment which seemed like a lifetime as it loaded, goading me, surely aware of my impatience and prolonging the torture.

I couldn't bear to read it; I hit print as fast as possible. Whatever the outcome, it wasn't real until it was physically in my hands.

How my legs supported my weight to the printer, I shall never know. The paper ripped as I desperately tore it from the machine, but there it was. The outcome. The final decision.

This is to certify that the named teacher has successfully completed…

Successfully completed. No more doubt. No more waiting. Seven years after my teacher training, I had finally completed the induction year. Not just completed… successfully completed. No more wondering about my career, about the implications of a failed induction forcing me out of the education system forever. I had completed it.

Tears burned my eyes as the realisation set in. It didn't matter what my teachers had said, or the former head-teacher who had made my life hell. Despite every attempt to knock my confidence and deter me, I had done it. The ghosts of my past no longer held power over me; neither my rape nor my miscarriage. I had developed a sense of compassion and an awareness of vulnerability, whether in spite of my past or because of it. I had lost my baby girl, but I still had the ability to change the lives of so many others for the better.

I had known from the instant I saw the email on my screen that this was a crossroads, something that would change my life forever, even though I wasn't sure of the direction it would take.

But it was more powerful than anyone could have realised.

I was no longer the girl who panicked or the girl who couldn't work with men. I wasn't the girl who couldn't be touched or the one who wasn't good enough.

For the first time in my life, I was the woman who could. The woman who could hold it together, the woman who could let people in. I was the woman who could teach and the woman who could achieve her dreams.

More importantly, I was finally reunited in myself; reunited in pride. My seven year old self who dreamt of teaching, the teenager who wasn't good enough. The girl who was raped and the mother who had lost her baby. The victim struggling to survive in a world that no longer made sense, and the young teacher who couldn't cope with the joint stresses of her job and her past.

I had always considered myself to be broken; fragile glass that had splintered and smashed apart and lay irreparable. But in that moment, all the fractured shards had been pieced back together, offering me a reflection, a true reflection of what I could be and what I had already become.

There were still scars, of course. There would always be

seams where the broken pieces had been restored. But the joins had been so carefully handled that they had become the strong bits. My strong bits.

In that moment, I realised that people believed in me, but – most importantly – I realised that I had begun to believe in myself.

I'm still at that school, where I felt so secure and cared for. I love being there and the community I am part of, but I'm also starting to gain the confidence to spread my wings and find a new adventure. Events can turn our lives upside down, leave us lost and vulnerable. But that doesn't have to be the end. It's still possible to achieve the dreams and break those chains. People can be rebuilt and thrive, not just survive.

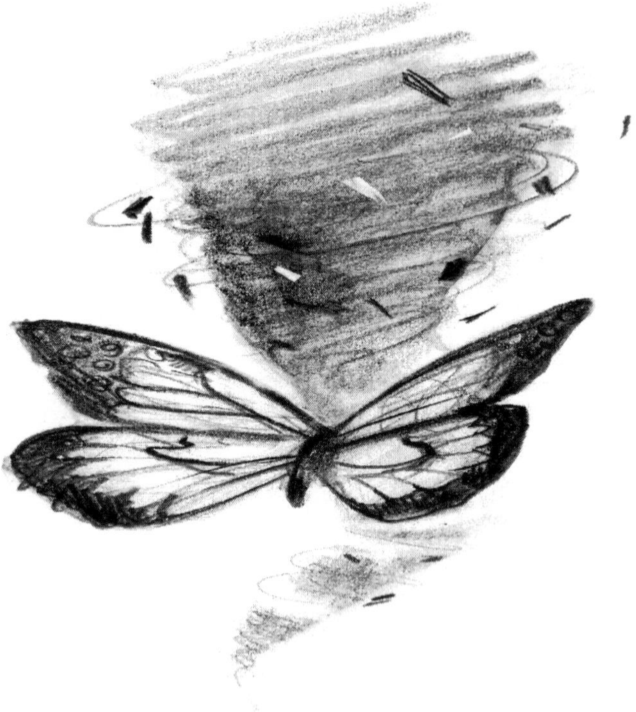

Turning Point
by Maureen Jeffs

"I love her, but I don't want the responsibility," he said. Mutely, I looked at this man, my husband. After my unloving, abusive childhood, I'd once believed he was someone to watch over me, as the old Gershwin song says. I was a naïve twenty-three year old when I met Paul; he nearly fifteen years older. Equating age with maturity, I'd invested him with qualities which he didn't possess as I realized once the first flush of love had faded. Over time it had dawned on me that I'd escaped the grip of a controlling mother only to find myself in the hands of a controlling man.

"You will look after her, won't you?" he continued.

Frozen in that moment, I watched raindrops misting the window behind him, heard the wind howling through the trees.

"If you won't have her, I'll have to ask those two retired nurses who used to look after her whenever Sue was away having ECT treatment."

I can't remember my answer. It must have included the word 'yes', because 'her', his fourteen year old daughter, Catherine, remained with me, her stepmother, after he drove off into the sunset with Linda, his mistress, in our family car.

Did Catherine cry into her pillow? Did she rant and rave when alone in her room? I don't know, I never asked, and now too many years have passed to pick at old sores. She said her dad told her she'd be better off with me as I'd probably remarry someone with money. Typical of my silver-tongued ex. My world had collapsed I was benumbed, operating on automatic. Childhood had taught me to hide my feelings behind an impenetrable, geisha-like mask.

He was still talking. "Linda's worried. She's afraid you'll go round and claw her eyes out. Can you reassure her?"

Did I tell him I wouldn't stoop so low? I may have. I

didn't want to see her, let alone touch her. I wasn't some fishwife who would behave like a participant on The Jeremy Kyle Show. I remembered when we all worked together at the swimming pool, which he was manager of, how he'd ridiculed her voice, her red hands – he had a thing about nice hands – and her habit of arriving at work with a head full of rollers ready for a night out. Now he was telling me how vulnerable she was, how she needed him, was earthy, whereas I had faults he couldn't live with. The faults that stick in my mind are having slimmed down to a size 10, and being a bluestocking – an intellectual or literary woman - as I'd begun to write poetry.

Paul was a charmer; he was also moody, proprietorial and mistrustful. I'd never given him any reason to doubt me because I wanted our relationship to be a forever thing, and for eight years I'd tried to build a secure world for Catherine, something she'd never had. Now he was kicking the foundations out from under us. I'm sure I made mistakes, who doesn't, but most of mine related to learning how to be a mother to a small girl, a girl who was only six when she'd found her mother, Sue, on the kitchen floor having committed suicide. At first Catherine and I had only one thing in common, in various ways we had both been damaged by our childhoods, but gradually love grew. I think I helped to repair her and I regarded her as my daughter. I wanted to be responsible for her; in fact I would have fought Paul in court to have care of her.

The financial aspects of the situation hadn't occurred to me, perhaps because much of life had assumed a surreal quality. One very important factor was that the house we lived in went with Paul's job. If he left the house and his job, Catherine and I would be offered alternative accommodation. I quickly discovered what that was; a shabby house on the outskirts of town, in an area where those who were considered undesirable lived. I still had some remnants of

Peace by Piece

pride; I was determined that Catherine and I were not going to live there. Another factor was Paul's job. As a swimming pool manager he came into contact with the public, many of whom were fellow students of Catherine. Since his betrayal, I was aware of people gossiping about us and realised it would be even more difficult for Catherine, a teenager. Life might be easier if we moved to another town. Couples splitting up is common now, but in 1973 it was more of an event. I knew I could expect no help from my family. My mother's only comment when I told her Paul intended to leave me, that our marriage had failed was, 'You would; just when your sister's about to get married'.

The chronology of events between Paul's announcement and the day he left are a blur, though some things stick in my mind. One evening, he came up behind me when he returned from work and fondled my arse.

"Leave me alone," I snapped, looking at his sweating, after-sex face, feeling physically sick. "Don't come from fooling about with her and think you can touch me."

This angered him. He shouted at me that I was still his wife then, in an attempt to hurt me, recounted some of his sexual encounters with Linda. A few months before our marriage broke down, he'd talked me into accompanying him on a hospital appointment. He wanted to have a vasectomy but the surgeon wouldn't perform the operation unless he had his wife's agreement. Unsure, but wanting to please him, I'd agreed to it. Now he was telling me that he'd had the vasectomy because Linda had told him she wouldn't have full sex with him until he'd had the operation. What a sucker I'd been. Before I'd recovered from that, he detailed an incident of sex with her on the floor of the swimming pool clubroom, including her orgasm. Like a punchbag, I sucked up the blows, bleeding inwardly.

Another event clearly recalled is my sister's wedding at which Catherine was a bridesmaid. I pasted on my best

121

Peace by Piece

smile, trying to appear normal. The sky was blue, the sun shone – perfect. I maintained my composure until I listened to the vows, promises which Paul and I had once made, and which I now knew were worthless on his part. I felt faint, I sweated inside my silk dress, I had an intense urge to rush out of the church. Somehow I held on. Afterwards when the photos were taken – I was not included in any of them – I watched Catherine, tense and pale faced in her high-necked, lilac dress. I knew she was suffering.

The day of Paul's departure arrived. A trivial detail comes to mind: he asked if he could take some of our towels with him, and I agreed. Then he was gone. I wanted to yell after him that he'd stolen my twenties, packed them in his case. I didn't; I'd learnt in my childhood to be silent when hurt. Whether or not he said goodbye to Catherine I can't recall. The mind doesn't operate as normal in traumatic situations.

Reality kicked in fast. There were bills to be paid. I soon discovered Paul had taken what little money we'd had in our joint account. There were no state benefits for one parent families in those days so I would have to leave my part-time job and find a full-time one.

Between Paul's announcement and the day he left, I'd become friendly
with James, who worked in the department responsible for the school I worked in.

He knew about my home situation as I'd mentioned it as the reason I needed to leave and look for full-time work. His visits to the school increased, and it dawned on me that his reasons for visiting were flimsy; he was coming to see me. One day, as he walked towards me down the school corridor, I realized I was becoming attracted to him too. I wasn't ready to begin a new relationship. I was fragile and mistrustful of men. James waited in the wings.

In my muddled thinking I came up with the idea to move to the mobile home park where Paul now lived. I reasoned

Peace by Piece

that unless Catherine lived nearby, he wouldn't bother to keep in contact with her. I've never been sure that was my only reason, and perhaps if I'd been mentally stronger at that time I'd have tested my theory out. My emotions were all over the place, but I no longer loved Paul. Any iota of love went down the toilet when he laughingly confessed that on our wedding day he'd been lusting after my friend, who was a witness. Maybe I wanted to rub in his face what he'd lost.

To raise money, I sold most of my furniture and some of my possessions. I sat mutely as strangers walked in and out of the house, clutching items, shoving money in my hand. To this day I regret selling a set of treasured encyclopaedia which had belonged to my grandmother.

You may know of Edward Lorenz's Chaos Theory, which says that when a butterfly flutters its wings in one part of the world, it can cause a hurricane in another. I never knew what the small event was that led one quiet afternoon to the hurricane that bowled me over. All I remember was suddenly being overwhelmed by my situation. I felt as if I was trapped in a bramble bush, thrashing around, unable to break free. I had to escape. Upstairs I had pills, hidden in the airing cupboard in my bedroom. What the pills were or when I'd seen my doctor who prescribed them, I can't recall. I think my memory has erased chunks of time from that period of my life. I do remember searching feverishly for them. I don't know if I would have taken them. I don't think so, but I can't be sure. At the moment my hand touched the container, the door burst open, a hand slapped my face and I slumped to the floor weeping. The hand that had struck me wiped my tears, put an arm round me, and led me to my friend Sally's home nearby. Apparently I had been talking with Sally earlier that afternoon and something I'd said had alarmed her. She'd shared her fears with her daughter, Karen, a trainee nurse, and asked her to check me.

"You'd locked yourself in your bedroom," Karen said.

"Sorry I had to slap you, but you were ..."
"I'm keeping your pills here and I've sent for your doctor," Sally said. "I'll sit with you until he arrives." She gave me a hug. "Don't worry. Karen will meet Catherine out of school. She can stay with us until the doctor leaves."

My doctor, Derek Cracknell, sat and talked with me for several hours. He

Told me I had much to live for, especially Catherine. I was ashamed that in my moment of madness I'd forgotten her. When I told him Paul had said his reason for leaving me was because I was too much of a bluestocking, he laughed wryly.

"Whatever they say, the reason most men leave their wives for is sex."

From that night I began not to be a reed shaken by the wind. I'd sunk to the bottom of a black pit, but I'd risen from it and knew I'd never sink so low again. Whenever I've had bad times since then – and there have been quite few, including being diagnosed with terminal cancer – I don't despair. I know I'll survive and find a window which the sun is shining through. May you find your window too.

***   I paused from writing this for a while. Thinking of that night, on impulse, I fed Derek Cracknell's name into Google. The first thing that appeared was his obituary. He died in August last year. Reading some of the words of one of his daughters, 'He would give anyone the time they needed ... often not returning from home visits until eleven or twelve at night', I found my eyes filling with tears. Once, I was one of those home visits. Six months too late to thank him, I only hope he realised how much he had helped me over forty years ago.

Peace by Piece

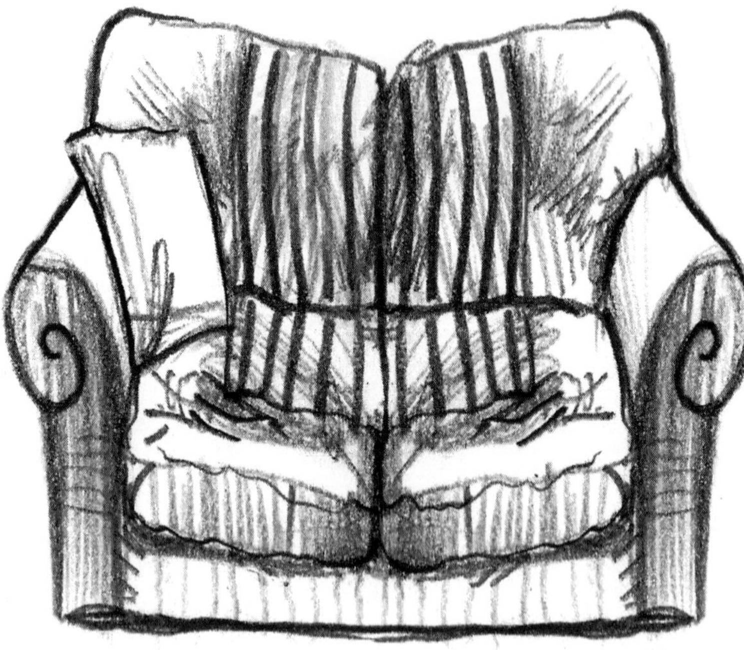

AN OLD BROWN SETTEE
by Andrea Agacinski

I was running up the stairs two at a time, totally focused on my mission.

The screech of my trainers on the highly polished wooden steps, together with the beat of my heart pounding in my ears, reminded me of the introduction to a well known piece of music.

It wasn't that I wanted to be right; however, surely it wasn't possible that I could be wrong? I felt quite angry as well as confused; it was a catch 22 situation. If he was telling me the truth then what would that make me, ignorant? But on the other hand, if he was winding me up, what would that mean? That that little flutter of excitement I had felt in my belly when he had first said it to me, which actually was still there, would soon be completely squashed.

At the top of the stairs, everything seemed normal. I'd been here lots of times, to this building that housed the books, CD's and videos, with its coffee shop and stationary department. I really liked it; it felt comfortable and warm. It had a great energy, making it a fabulous place to meet with friends or simply be on my own with a coffee.

To my right was the coffee shop, busy as always. The strong aroma of beans from all around the world mixed with the sweetness of all the flavourings tempted my nostrils, causing them to twitch. I knew that it was busy because of the monotonous buzz of people like a drone of bees working tirelessly in their hive. Usually, I would look towards the window, to assess whether my favourite table was patiently waiting for me. Today, however, I had no intention of idling over coffee, I was on a mission!

Over my right shoulder were the lovely, lumpy old brown leather settees, cracked like the parched earth of a dried up river bed, sagging in different places after years of bottoms of all sizes sitting on them. They were so familiar to me that I knew which particular cushions not to sit on, unless you wanted to either sink in further than expected and spill your coffee on the way down, or have some kind of alien finger, hidden in the leather, prod you indignantly as you sat on it.

And there, to my left, were the rows and rows of books. Books on every subject you could think of. I stopped abruptly, like a car engaging in an emergency stop, not giving a second thought to the people behind me. The screeching stopped with me but my heart seemed to have intensified its pounding.

A thought had just popped into my mind; I couldn't actually ask anyone, could I? If it was a wind up, I would look and feel such a fool. I thought about the time a comedian of a friend of mine had asked my daughter to bring back some tinned bananas from the supermarket, and how upset she had been when she came home after realising it was a joke. It's funny how random thoughts simply barge their way into our minds without being invited.

OK...so I would just have to search myself, wouldn't I?

Well one thing I knew for sure, was that IF there were any of these books they wouldn't be in the self-development section. I would have seen them already, because it was my favourite corner of the entire building and I had invested many hours browsing amongst those fascinating titles, drawn to them either by size or colour or, sometimes, by something ethereal.

I decided to be guided by the alphabet; I needed the "H" section.

That drew a blank.

My mood and excitement were dropping. The anticipation had subsided, the fluttering in my tummy had died and I could no longer hear my heart. It was an inconclusive search.

Because disappointment had thrown itself over me, like

a heavy net that captures an unsuspecting victim, I found myself heading towards the section I liked the best.

It was only in the past 3 years that I had been introduced to "self-development." I had never heard of it before, but I knew I found it all to be so very exciting! Some of it I read over and over again, some I didn't understand, some I had to question. But what I did come to realise, was that it was OK, because the key word in this, was "self" and that, for me, meant that it was about *me*.

As a child, a teenager and young adult I didn't like reading. I truly didn't get why some people actually enjoyed it. I don't think it ever dawned on me that perhaps they were reading things they actually enjoyed or were interested in.

But since my first encounter with this self-development stuff, I couldn't read fast enough and I had invested lots of money in books. I'd had to buy two bookcases to house them all and because I was buying them faster than I could read them I decided that one was my "self-development" bookcase, which contained the books that I had read, scribbled over and highlighted in bright yellow and orange, and the other was my "shelf-development" bookcase. These books were still all shiny and their pages were tightly pressed together, like the bud of a flower patiently waiting to open. These were the books that I had yet to delve into, to absorb the knowledge hidden inside.

The coffee shop was getting busier. Or was it that I had now tuned into it because my mood had deflated? I don't know, but just as I was having these thoughts, I saw exactly what had bought me there.

LOTS OF THEM! And they *were* in my favourite section, that I had looked at many times before. Someone must have only just put them there that day. They couldn't possibly have been there all along?

Books on happiness! I'm sure my mouth was gaping like

a fish gasping for oxygen. He was telling me the truth! There really are books on happiness! My eyes went along the line:
The Secrets of Happy People...Happiness Now...The Art of Happiness...The Science of Happiness...What Happy People Know...How to Make Yourself Happy...
I stared at the people who were all doing their own thing inside the coffee shop. Groups of mums with their babies, laughing, (that doesn't necessarily mean they are happy though, does it?) The guy focused on his laptop; (nice suit, must earn a lot of money, but does that mean he's happy?) That group of young girls giggling together, probably discussing the latest boys, (are they happy?) What is happiness? And how do we know when we are?

"Excuse me!" I bellowed as loud as I could. "Do you people know that there are books on happiness? That you can study it?"

The response was silence; everyone ignored me, carrying on with whatever they were doing.

Only I had heard the question, though, because it was my mind that had shouted it out, not my voice. Surely I couldn't be the only person who thought you either were happy or you weren't, depending on what happened to you? Oh my God, is it really a choice?

I carefully chose a couple of books, unconsciously wandered over to my old brown settee and slowly sat down. It let out a deep, tired sigh, as if to complain about my weight. Randomly, I opened the first one and started to read, and it made me laugh:"Some cause happiness wherever they go; others whenever they go," Oscar Wilde.

As I read, that exciting feeling in my tummy started to bubble up again.

A few hours earlier, I had been with my inspirational friend Ian. He and I spent lots of time discussing all sorts of subjects and I was always learning from him. I had been

telling him about my friend Sue and how unhappy she was. Our conversation went like this:
"Why is she unhappy?"
"I dunno." I sighed. "According to her, she has no idea."
"Why do you think she's unhappy?"
I shrugged. "That's how it works, isn't it? Some people are and some aren't, that's just the way it is."
"Is that how it works?"
I stared at him. I recognised the tone he'd used. It was the tone he'd used many times before, the one that gave me permission to question something that I believed to be the truth.
"If your friend wanted to learn to speak Spanish, what could she do?"
"Learn, obviously, by studying it."
He smiled.
"Study happiness?" I said, slowly. "Learn to be happy? Are you serious?"
He raised his eyebrows.
"How"? I screeched, sounding distinctly owl-like.
"She could start with a book."

And that's why I'm here, sitting on this old, familiar, brown settee, with my life about to turn in a totally new direction.
How could I be fifty-two years old and not know that you can study happiness? That we can learn about what it is and how it works?
How can those books have been in the section I had looked at many times, yet I'd never seen them?
How many other people don't know that happiness can be a choice?
I gently closed the book, leaned back and shut my eyes. Now there were lots of questions floating around in my mind like bubbles blown from a tub by a child.
In that moment I started to feel that familiar flutter start

Peace by Piece

to bubble up again in my tummy.

Choice; what if there is always a choice but sometimes we simply don't know it? Maybe we just don't always see it?

I thought about something I had read recently.

"We don't see what our eyes show us, we see what we believe."

I wasn't looking for those books before. I didn't know or believe they existed. Is that why I didn't see them?

Maybe I should start to question everything from now on?

I thought about something else I had read.

"We don't know what we don't know."

If we don't know something, how can we change it?

Sue wasn't happy, but she didn't know why. If she knew there were books to help her learn how to be happy, then at least she would have a choice, instead of believing that it had to be that way. It simply had never entered her mind to question it.

Now there's another profound question in my head. Why do we accept things as being the truth and not think to question them?

Almost immediately, I had a possible answer.

It went back to when my daughters were very little. All three of them went through a stage where they were constantly asking WHY over and over and over again, and at first I would answer, and then I'd get fed up and my answer would change to something like, "Because I said so." And then I'd end up saying, "Stop asking why!"

I sat in silence.

So that's it. Like lots of other people, I was probably conditioned to accept other people's reality and truth as my own and never think to question it.

In that moment my life changed. I was now in charge of me, my life, my direction and my decisions.

No other person, only me.

Peace by Piece

And do you know what? I question everything.
And do you know what else? It's so much more fun!

Peace by Piece

global words

Global Words CIC is a social enterprise which provides an all-encompassing service for all writers, ranging from basic proofreading to full ghost writing and typesetting. Our community focussed work involves delivering writing projects to underserved and under-represented groups across Nottinghamshire.

To learn more about Global Words, visit:
www.globalwords.co.uk

Other books also by Global Words Press:

Speaking OUT: LGBTQ Youth Memoirs
Late OutBursts: LGBTQ Memoirs